July 2017

YOU CAN HAVE A
DOG WHEN I'M DEAD

YOU CAN HAVE A DOG WHEN I'M DEAD

Essays on Life at an Angle

• •

PAUL BENEDETTI

DUNDURN
TORONTO

Cover image: Li Kim Goh/iStock
Printer: Webcom

Library and Archives Canada Cataloguing in Publication

Benedetti, Paul, author
      You can have a dog when I'm dead : essays on life at an angle / Paul Benedetti.

Issued in print and electronic formats.
ISBN 978-1-4597-3811-9 (softcover).--ISBN 978-1-4597-3812-6 (PDF).--
ISBN 978-1-4597-3813-3 (EPUB)

      I. Title. II. Title: You can have a dog when I am dead.

PS8603.E55627Y59 2017   C814.6   C2016-906904-4
                                                C2016-906903-6

3   4   5   21   20   19   18   17

Conseil des Arts du Canada   Canada Council for the Arts

Canada

ONTARIO ARTS COUNCIL
CONSEIL DES ARTS DE L'ONTARIO
an Ontario government agency
un organisme du gouvernement de l'Ontario

We acknowledge the support of the **Canada Council for the Arts** and the **Ontario Arts Council** for our publishing program. We also acknowledge the financial support of the **Government of Ontario**, through the **Ontario Book Publishing Tax Credit** and the **Ontario Media Development Corporation**, and the **Government of Canada**.

Care has been taken to trace the ownership of copyright material used in this book. The author and the publisher welcome any information enabling them to rectify any references or credits in subsequent editions.
                                                — *J. Kirk Howard, President*

The publisher is not responsible for websites or their content unless they are owned by the publisher.

Printed and bound in Canada.

VISIT US AT

dundurn.com | @dundurnpress | dundurnpress | dundurnpress

Dundurn
3 Church Street, Suite 500
Toronto, Ontario, Canada
M5E 1M2

Contents

Introduction

Like a lot of things in life, this book really began over a beer.

It was December 2007 when my pal Dave Estok invited me out for a drink. About a year earlier, Dave had returned to his hometown newspaper, *The Hamilton Spectator*, as its new editor-in-chief. Dave and I had spent years at the paper together in the early 1980s as young reporters, and had remained close friends ever since.

After our first beer and the usual catching up, Dave asked me if I'd like to write for the paper again. I was teaching journalism full time and still freelancing. I had written some short personal essays — sometimes funny, sometimes not — for the *Globe and Mail*, a short-lived magazine called *Ruby*, and *Canadian Living*, and really enjoyed it. So I was interested but cautious.

"What do you want me to write?" I asked.

"A column," he said.

"About what?" I asked.

"Whatever you want," he said.

"Whatever I want?"

"Yes," he said.

In journalism and organized crime, this is known as "an offer you can't refuse."

"I don't want to write about city politics, quirky characters, or serious issues of any kind," I said. "You have people who do that better than me already."

"I know," he said. "Write about your life."

So I did.

I wrote about my wife, my kids, my parents, and my neighbours, about getting older, not much wiser but a bit fatter, about losing my keys and losing my mind. I wrote about birthdays and bar mitzvahs, about first babies and baptisms, and about weddings and wakes. I wrote about kids staying and then about them leaving, about wishing they would go and then missing them like crazy. I wrote about remembering, but more often forgetting — everything from my anniversary to my wallet. And sometimes I wrote about dying, but more often I just wrote about living, about how I was bumbling through my own life, doing the best I could.

That usually meant making fun of myself and of life. But often it gave me the chance to stop and reflect on things a bit, too.

So, now when people ask me, "What do you write about?" I say, "Nothing. And everything."

So that's what the essays in this book are about — nothing and everything.

I hope you like it.

• • • • •

You may be wondering about the title: *You Can Have a Dog When I'm Dead*. It's also about life, a reference to our ongoing discussion about getting a dog. My wife wants one; I don't. I think all good marriages are based on compromise.

That's mine.

Paul Benedetti
September 2016

My Kingdom for a Good Night's Sleep

June 17, 1999

Lately, I have been sleeping with two women. I mean, two women simultaneously. That is, I have two women in my bed at night. Now under most circumstances this would be considered quite a good thing. In fact, most guys I know would consider this quite excellent and want to hear details. Not so in this case.

You see, the two women are my wife and my two-year-old daughter. The former I am quite used to sleeping with, and have done so every night with few exceptions for the past eleven years. It's my daughter who's the problem.

It's not like she doesn't have her own bed and has to sleep with us. She has a perfectly nice bed; hell, she's got her own room and, frankly, it's bigger than ours. I pointed this out to my wife when we were getting it ready for the new baby and she gave me a look that said, "Only a selfish, uncaring lout would even talk about room size at a time like this." I've never actually heard my wife use the word *lout*, but I'm pretty sure she was thinking it.

Anyway, back to the sleeping arrangements. It's not like I'm not used to this. We have three children and the two older boys also migrated to our bed during the night. Somehow, that didn't seem as much of a bother. Maybe it was because I was younger. Maybe, because I was a new (and then newish) father, I thought it was cute. This happens for a while and is probably the reason you don't mind being barfed on in public and other fun dad experiences. Or maybe it was because the boys were just less trouble. I'm not sure. A good part of those years is a fog, and believe me it wasn't due to drinking. When you're helping raise two young boys, you don't really need booze to be dazed and confused.

But my daughter, Ella (who is extremely cute, I must admit), is a complete pain in bed. For one thing she's constantly throwing off the sheet and blankets. I don't blame her; her little body is like some kind of thermonuclear reactor. Apparently, according to scientific research, a child's metabolism is so fast that they give off enough heat to run a small steam turbine. (Okay, I made that up, but you get the point.) Whatever the reason, her antics leave me uncovered and shivering in the middle of the night.

She also likes to roll around, press her feet against me, and lie on my head. Why anyone, even a two-year-old kid, would find sleeping on my head comfortable is not entirely clear, but judging by how soundly she sleeps while on my head, it's obvious that she does.

About halfway through the night, my long-suffering wife usually gives up and migrates to my daughter's bed. I would do that myself, except I am six feet tall and after one night of sleeping in Ella's bed, I woke up in the morning ready for the lead in *Richard III*.

Once my daughter discovers that my wife has left (she seems to have some kind of built-in parent radar that wakes her up if we're not being annoyed enough), she follows her back to her own bed and hops in. That means that moments later, they both arrive back in bed with me and the whole rigmarole starts again.

All of this would be almost tolerable except that my daughter adds to the torture by occasionally peeing on us. You just haven't lived until you wake up at 4:30 a.m. shivering in a bed drenched with ice-cold kid pee. It makes filling out your tax form look good. For some reason (and it could be my hot-kid-body theory) being drenched in pee doesn't seem to bother Ella. Oh no, she's wet and warm and sound asleep by this point.

So, my wife and I get up, and in a zombie-like state, strip the bed, put on fresh sheets, and plop back in, our daughter once again firmly wedged between us. (What's the sense of moving her now, she's pretty much done everything she can to us.)

After one hour of sleep, the alarm goes off and we're awake, fully rested and energized for another day at work. My wife gets up and heads for her morning bath, and as soon as Ella hears the water (kid radar again), she trundles in and joins her in the tub. Of course, I feel sorry for my poor wife. But that leaves me — for about fifteen minutes — alone in a queen-size bed.

Believe me, it's pure bliss.

Handy? Me? Well, I Do Have a Toolbox …

February 27, 2006

My brother-in-law set up and cabled our new computer. My other brother-in-law fixed our blocked kitchen sink drain. My sister-in-law just finished renovating our upstairs bathroom. I certainly could have done all these things myself. I could have, if I had any actual skills. Or tools. But, as a matter of fact, I have neither.

I do have a toolbox. My wife's father used to manufacture toolboxes, so I got one as a wedding present. I was hoping for a new house or a thick envelope of cash, but the toolbox was a nice yellow colour, so I said thanks and began to drink heavily at the reception.

I have many things in the toolbox: wire, some old fuses, a light switch, several door handles, a lot of loose screws, a fishing lure, and some metal things that could be pretty much anything. But no tools.

There are several screwdrivers scattered around the house in drawers and cupboards. I had a hammer once in the mid-nineties. I have no power tools (I still have all my fingers. I feel there is a direct correlation between these facts.)

I come by all of this naturally. My father was not what you would call "handy." He pretty much wore a suit all the time. He wore one grocery shopping. I think for several years during my childhood, he slept in a suit. He had no workshop, no workbench. He didn't even have a toolbox. The few tools he had are still in a coffee can in the garage. I think he last used them during the Trudeau years.

As a result, I really don't know anything about household repairs. I actually don't know anything about how our house even works.

A few years ago, we had friends over for the weekend, and over a beer Doug, who runs a heating and air conditioning company in Toronto, asked me about my furnace.

"What about it?" I said.

"Well, when's the last time you checked the filter?" he said.

I panicked. Furnaces have filters? I thought they just warmed up the house. I didn't know they were like giant air Britas. I mean, who knew?

"I didn't know they had filters," I said. Doug knows that I don't know anything, so there was no sense pretending.

We went downstairs. The thing he pulled out of the furnace looked like a grey angora throw pillow. "It's a bit dirty. We should change it," he said.

"Into what?" I asked.

"We should put in a new one. Where do you keep them?" he asked.

It was then that I realized there were people who have shelves in their basements where new furnace filters sat neatly stacked waiting to be used. This seemed quite unbelievable to me, like dogs talking or someone who really wants to luge.

I admitted everything — that I had never actually looked at the furnace. I just assumed that as long as I could hear a humming noise in the basement and the children were not covered in frost every morning that things were okay. I had noticed that there seemed to be an inordinate amount of grit in the house, but I just thought that was because we lived in Hamilton.

On Monday, a huge box of furnace filters arrived at my front door. Earlier, Doug had shown me how to install them and with a magic marker had drawn an arrow on the furnace to make sure I did not put them in backwards, which would have had me filtering the neighbourhood air. He knows me well.

I realize that most men would find this incident humiliating. I, on the other hand, saw it as a moment of discovery. Most guys love to show that they know how things work — cars, furnaces, air conditioners, computers, lawnmowers, the federal banking system, you name it. All I had to do was present the opportunity for them and the rest would take care of itself.

That's all I do now. Recently I called my neighbour Phil over to "take a look at something." We had bought a heavy new mirror and it needed to be anchored into the wall studs. This required a stud finder, a power drill, several screw inserts, and a moderate level of intelligence. This ruled me out. As I opened beers and chatted, Phil hung the mirror.

My other technique is to invite people over for dinner. I may not know a Robertson from a Phillips (okay, I memorized those names to impress the guys at Home Depot), but I can prepare a decent plate of osso bucco and risotto Milanese. Once they're here, I say something like, "Can you take a look at this ceiling fan. I just can't seem to get it working." Of course, I haven't even tried to get it working, but hey, they don't know that.

A half-hour later my fan is fixed.

I think this system will do the trick for a long time. When it ceases to work, I will talk my wife into taking a home renovation course at night school.

Want a Lift to the Gym?

April 17, 2006

My friend is a recovering kid-drive-aholic. He announced this to me the other day.

He said it the way people say really big things like: "I'm going to climb Mount Everest" or "I've decided to floss daily."

He told me that as of next week he's not driving his kids to school anymore. That's it.

"I'm sick of all the waiting and yelling and hassle in the morning. They can walk to school from now on," he said, or words to that effect. I wasn't taking notes because I was in a state of shock.

Of course, that was nothing compared to the shock the kids felt. How would they get to school? It could take almost fifteen minutes of walking to get from our street to the high school. Actual walking. They were pretty freaked out. Would they need water? An energy bar? Special shoes? They weren't sure. And their friends couldn't help them — many had never walked before.

"This is not going to be easy," I said. "There's going to be a lot of pressure — and not just from your kids." But he seemed confident. In the face of the unthinkable — not driving your kids wherever they want to go — he appeared strong. When word got out, he would become a pariah, of course.

I'm not sure exactly when it became the duty of parents to drive their kids everywhere. It just sort of crept up on us, like twenty-dollar allowances and four-hundred-dollar iPods. Suddenly, and without warning, you were a lazy, even negligent parent, if you didn't chauffeur your kid anywhere anytime, day or night. I do remember the first time during a dinner party that a cellphone went off and a guest had to leave to pick up Suzy or Johnny at the movies. I remember thinking, "How did it come to this?" but I stayed quiet.

I don't know how it started, but one thing I'm sure of is that it didn't start with our parents. Listen, my dad never drove me anywhere. He didn't drive me to school. He didn't drive me to basketball practice in the morning. He didn't drive me to games at night. He didn't drive me to art lessons. He never drove me to go bowling or to the Saturday movies. I think he would have refused to drive us on our summer vacations if he could have found a way around it.

My father was not a mean person. He was busy. He left for work about 6:30 a.m. every morning. He didn't get back until about 6:30 or later at night. We only had one car. Even if we'd had two, my mother didn't drive. And the idea of asking my dad, who had just come home from another twelve-hour day, to drive me anywhere never really entered my mind. Good thing it didn't, either, because he would have laughed out loud at the idea.

"Dad, I was wondering if you could stop reading the paper, put down your drink, and drive me and four friends to see *The Poseidon Adventure*?"

"Sure, Paul. When do you need to be picked up? I'll stay up. And would you like me to clean your room while you're out?"

No, my dad was not available for chauffeur duty. In fact, I didn't know anyone whose dad who drove them anywhere. You wanted to go somewhere, you walked or took the bus. I know kids who have never set foot on a city bus. They must think they're giant RVs for old ladies.

Okay, it's not true that my dad never drove me anywhere. The last summer of high school I had a shot at getting a job in the newsroom of CBC Radio in Toronto as a copy boy. It was a big deal. My dad dropped me off at the bus stop in Aldershot and wished me luck. I hopped on the first GO Bus that showed up. I dozed off and when I opened my eyes and glanced out the window, I thought, Gee, Toronto sure looks a lot like Hamilton. When I saw the familiar white marble of City Hall go by,

I knew I might be in a bit of trouble. I called home. "Can you drive me to Toronto?" I said.

"I just drove you to the bus stop," he said.

"I know, but I took the bus back to Hamilton."

What he said after that was a colourful mix of Italian and English words that involved something called a pig-dog, Christopher Columbus, and a couple of extremely difficult physical acts. That day, at high speed, my dad gave me a ride to downtown Toronto. I was late, but the interview went well and I got the job. I was very thankful he drove me that day and I'm pretty sure I never asked my father for another ride in my life.

So, when did everything change? I don't know. But I know that almost all parents are worried because too many children today are overweight. We complain that kids don't get enough exercise. And what do we do to help them?

We drive them to the gym.

Hospital Daze: What I Learned This Summer

August 25, 2004

You can learn a lot sitting around a hospital. Not that I recommend it as a way of furthering your education. Taking a nice community college course would be better and, given what hospitals charge for parking, probably cheaper, but a hospital stay offers an education in itself.

For example, I learned that if you are the least bit distracted, you can lose your car virtually every day in an underground parking lot. I also learned that almost everyone in Canada is driving a van that is an indistinguishable blue-grey-green colour. Finally, I found out why some people have a huge and usually bizarre ("I climbed Mount Rainier and vomited") bumper sticker. They may be embarrassed, but at least they can find their van.

We were at the hospital because our fifteen-year-old son went in for corrective back surgery. He had a curved spine, which made him appear to be permanently slouching. Although this look is pretty much universal among teenagers, it isn't something you want to have your whole life.

The surgeons told us they could fix it and they did. It took nine-and-a-half hours on the operating table and ten days in hospital, but our son now stands straight and is, amazingly, three inches taller.

I'd call it a miracle, but when you see the work the doctors and nurses put into such a procedure, you know that if a deity is involved, it's only as an unpaid consultant.

So, what do you learn when you have to spend ten long days and even longer nights in the hospital?

Well, you find out, as you leaf through five-year-old copies of *Reader's Digest*, that little has changed. People are still telling you how to survive a bear attack and, if you live, how to save a million for retirement. On reflection, I figured that they are equally implausible.

You will discover that, given enough incentive, you'll wash your hands about four hundred times a day. Dozens of posters about horrible pathogens that could invade the human body convinced me that EPH (extreme personal hygiene) was a good idea. I pumped enough alcohol-based disinfectant gel on my hands to kill every known organism in the universe, or at least give them one hell of a hangover.

In light of that, I can't believe anyone in the hospital ever shakes hands with anyone else. The doctors do it, but I noticed they're always wearing gloves and masks.

After one night, you'll figure out that the only people who can get any sleep at the hospital are getting regular doses of morphine. There are enough monitors and machines beeping, squeaking, dinging, ringing to keep a narcoleptic alert. If a patient does manage to doze off, a well-meaning nurse will bustle in moments later to check one or more bodily functions. This goes on until morning, when, if the patient is at last getting a little sleep, someone nicely wakes him up for breakfast.

You will not be surprised that hospital food is bad. Perhaps food is the wrong word. I think "food objects" best describes what arrives on the trays. Sure, the things look like toast or an omelette or even some kind of meat, but they're actually playdough models made by kids in the nearby arts-and-crafts room.

You'll learn that the complaining, sullen teenager you have at home can turn into a courageous and stoic young man when he has to. You'll see him walk down a hall and into an operating room filled with monitors and surgical tools, and not flinch. You'll see a brave smile on his face and feel his hand squeeze yours as if to comfort you, even as the mask goes over his face and he fades off into unconsciousness.

You'll find out that your wife will call her children, no matter how big and grown-up they become, "my babies," and that that's okay.

You will understand, as you walk past the rooms on the pediatric ward, your eyes darting to the children lying in their beds, that there are many kids in the world who are damaged and broken and sick, and that not all of them will get well.

You'll learn that while most parents are driving their sons and daughters to swimming or soccer every day, other mothers and fathers are sitting and pacing and waiting to find out if things are getting better or worse for their child.

You will realize that you are lucky and you may think that once a year, everyone should have to take a long, slow walk through a hospital ward.

You'll discover that you really don't mind watching *Wayne's World* again and that *Old School* makes you laugh out loud despite yourself, and that sitting around in a small room isn't so bad as long as you know your kid is getting stronger every day and soon he'll be home again.

Finally, you'll learn, if you are thinking at all, that life is pretty good and the things that were bugging you — your overdrawn bank account, your shrinking RRSPs, and whatever that stuff is that's infested the front lawn — don't matter very much after all.

That's well worth learning.

Brotherly Love

June 5, 2006

A few weeks ago I found my son Matthew sleeping on the floor beside his big brother James's bed. He was curled up on a thin blue camping pad with his sleeping bag half over him. I could see his feet, dirty white socks still on them, sticking out over the end of the pad.

I had gone that night to check on James. He was recovering from major surgery and my wife and I would go down into the basement every few hours to look in on him and make sure everything was okay. This is not as easy as it sounds.

A few years ago we made the decision to move the bedrooms of our two teenage boys into the basement. We renovated, built them their own bathroom, and they've been down there ever since. (Okay, they come up for school, meals, and to ask for money, but that's about it.) So, going down there is a bit of a cross between a visit to African Lion Safari and New Orleans after the hurricane.

Most of the time you can't actually see the floor. It's just a sea of pizza boxes, video game cases, pop cans, running shoes, chip bags, socks, Slurpee containers, dirty dishes, and a host of unidentifiable objects. You know things are moving because you can hear the rustling and squeaking. I always say to myself, "Please, god, let it be the guinea pigs," but because I can't readily see their cage among the squalor, I'm never really sure. Over the past few years, we've tried to clean up down there, but the cost of the full-body environmental suits and the Scott Air-Paks means we don't do it very often.

In any case, I made it through the debris to James's room. About a month shy of his seventeenth birthday, he had gone into hospital for the third surgery on his back. In early adolescence, some kids — mostly girls — get scoliosis, a condition where the spine curves and twists to the right or the left. James had a version of this that bent his spine forward, the way age often stoops the elderly.

This time, two surgeons worked to straighten James's back, installing a complicated array of screws, hooks, and metal rods along his spinal vertebrae. They had to operate through the front and the back and it took eighteen hours and three shifts of nurses to do the job. When the doctors came out of the operating room, just after one in the morning, they were flushed and beaming. It had gone well — long, but well — and they were happy with what they had been able to do. "He's got a Cadillac in there now," said the lead surgeon.

We were happy, but we knew it would be a long road back for James. He was in the intensive care unit, intubated and sedated, for five days. After that, he spent close to two weeks in the children's ward, the "boy-man" among the babies and toddlers there. It would be days before James, with help, could even sit up. And more days would pass before, with a physiotherapist by his side, he would take a few tentative steps, his IV stand rolling beside him. These brief excursions would leave him bathed in sweat, ready for more painkillers and a long rest.

This kind of surgery requires almost a year to "take," as the bone grafts grow and secure the rods into place. It means that James can only sit, stand, and walk for the next months, while his body heals from the inside. He knows that, and he has done it before and will do it again. But he did not, and cannot, do it without help. And neither can we.

If there is, as people always say, some unexpected good in the most difficult of challenges, in this one it was the outpouring of kindness and help from the people around us. One of my wife's sisters, Sandy, flew up from Florida and moved into our house for a month to help us. Our siblings, our parents, friends, relatives, work colleagues, and neighbours called and wrote, visited at the hospital, and came to the house. They dropped off home-cooked meals, food baskets, magazines and books, teddy bears, and get-well cards.

And down in the basement, Matthew, who is fourteen, would sit with James, silently play computer games while he slept, and bring him a cool drink when he needed it. At night, Matthew, who sleeps one room over, was worried that he would not be able to hear James call out for help. So, without saying anything to us, he left his own bed, and quietly lay down beside his brother. Late in the night, he would help James go to the bathroom or fetch him a glass of water. Sometimes, half-awake, he would come to tell us James needed more medication for his pain.

A few weeks have passed, and with each day James gets a little better. His progress is slow but steady. A few days ago, with his brother by his side, he walked all the way around the block. And each morning, when I go down to wake Matthew up for school, I find him there, asleep beside his big brother's bed. I asked Matthew how long he was going to stay on the floor in James room. He looked at me, thought about it for a minute and said, "Until he doesn't need me anymore."

We hope that will be soon — and never.

Underwear? Under the Tree, of Course!

October 4, 2006

It's the holiday season and unlike most people, I am looking forward to the traditional gift of underwear and socks. In fact, I'm almost giddy with anticipation over the prospect of new underwear. I need new underwear. Not desperately, but there is the odd morning when even I am aware that the Joe Boxers I am slipping into have seen better days.

"You're going to wear those?" my wife says, looking over at me getting dressed. She makes a face not unlike the one she uses when she opens the lid of the green cart.

"Who's going to see them?" I say, falling back on an argument I used when I was six.

"No one, I hope, but still, they're pretty ratty. There's holes in them."

There are holes in my underwear, but they're not so big that there's any danger of "accidental body part escape" and anyway, the ventilation is, well, kind of pleasant.

"You can't wear those. Come on," she says.

I check the underwear drawer. It is, like I will be shortly, bare.

"Well, here's the choice: this pair of flannel Mickey Mouse shorts I got a decade ago as some kind of twisted birthday gift or I could try to wear this Crown Royal bag."

I demonstrate how I might adapt the Crown Royal bag as underwear. It's not a pretty sight.

"Okay, never mind, but you've got to get some new underwear."

Easier said than done. For one thing, I don't seem to have the time to go underwear shopping anymore. Sure, in the old days before marriage and kids, I would routinely while away the weekend browsing through the racks of Stanfields and Jockeys with glee. Okay, that's a bit of an exaggeration. Let's face it, overly enthusiastic underwear shopping would likely attract store security.

Underwear seemed more important then. There was an underwear revolution underway. Calvin Klein and Joe Boxer were breaking new, uncharted ground in the world of advanced underwear design. People talked about it. I wrote articles about it. Hell, PBS did a miniseries on it — or was it on the Civil War? I can never remember. Anyway, underwear was also more important then because there was the off chance that a woman you didn't know all that well might see them. And I don't mean a nurse in the emergency room. In my case, the probabilities of that happening were closer to the chances of winning the lottery or hearing an intelligent comment on a radio phone-in show, but that's neither here nor there now.

I also think underwear were easier to buy then.

Recently, I tried to find a pair when I took my ten-year-old daughter shopping at the mall. By the way, there's a dangerous pastime. It's pretty hard to remain conscious, never mind amuse yourself, looking at four hundred different hair scrunchies while your kids tries to pick three-for-ten-dollar earring sets from a wall that has nine thousand different kinds. Is every man, woman, and child in China busy all day making plastic preteen fashion accessories? Who's left to build the important things like nuclear reactors and illegal knock-off Olympics bags and hats?

Anyway, I finally made it to the men's underwear section of a major department store, which shall remain nameless but is called The Bay. Of course, by this point I had almost no money left, having bought a bag load of cheap accessories and a lunch — and at the mall a slice of pizza and a pop cost the same as a large, fully-loaded pizza delivered to your house.

More problematic than my lack of funds though was the undergarment section itself. There had to be about 112 kinds of underwear to choose from. Knee-length, thigh-length, form-fitted, baggy, boxers, jockeys, coloured, patterned, low-rise, high-rise, and even strangely small bikini-style underwear disturbingly similar to the micro–bathing suits worn by aging overweight German tourists who somehow always make it into the background of your holiday beach photos. Hasn't anyone told the German government that Speedos belong on Olympic swimmers and that thongs should never be worn by a man under any circumstances ever?

I finally found some underwear that seemed okay. Until I looked at the price. Wow, since when did underwear cost as much as a case of beer? No wonder a lot of guys don't bother.

Worse than the price was the pricing formula. I know Canadians like to buy on sale, but you need a calculator and Stephen Hawking with you to figure out the real cost of any particular item. The sign above the underwear said "Buy More—Save More!" and in brackets "And Get More and More Confused Until You Get Dizzy and Fall Down." It was 30 percent off on one, 40 percent on two, and 50 percent on four or more but only on three particular brands and only on Saturday and only if your last name started with a letter between J and Q. Even the woman at the counter couldn't figure it out. Does a package of two pair of underwear count as one or two? Neither of us could remember what brands were on sale, the checkout was about a half-mile away from the underwear racks, and there were a dozen people behind me all clutching equally confusing on-sale products. The old flannel Mickey Mouse shorts were starting to look good.

I abandoned the underwear at the counter. I will wait for Christmas and I will be truly happy when I tear through the wrapping paper and find underwear. As long as they're not thongs.

"It's Not Muskoka"

January 2008

We have a cottage on the shores of Lake Erie. If people ask me to describe it I sometimes say, "It's not Muskoka."

Muskoka is the well-known cottage district north of Toronto where, among others, hockey players and movie stars have their cottages, if you call something with thirty rooms, five fireplaces, two boathouses, and a swimming pool, a cottage.

No, ours is a real cottage-cottage. It sits, a bit precariously, on the banks of Peacock Point, a tiny spit of land that pokes out a little ways into the vastness of Lake Erie. If you could jump on the back of a seagull and fly due south across the lake you would eventually arrive in Erie, Pennsylvania, though why you would want to do that is beyond me.

Our cottage began as a hunting shack in the 1920s for my wife's Irish grandfather and his pals, who came out to the point to shoot deer and, I suspect, drink a fair bit of whisky. Over the years they added a room here and there to house the ever-increasing number of children and grandchildren. Eventually, the aging wooden structure began to crumble and one winter a family of raccoons decided to make it home. That next spring we tore down the old place and, joining forces with my wife's sister and her husband, built a new cottage.

Just to be clear, this is not the cottage country of majestic pines and the haunting call of the loon at midnight. It's more a country of lawn gnomes, swing sets, and the not infrequent roar of Harley-Davidsons at two in the morning. But it has its charm. There is an old-fashioned Peacock Point General Store just down the laneway that serves coffee in the morning and dishes out ice cream cones and penny candy for the kids. Nearby is the community park with its teeter-totters and horseshoe pit and enough room to have a pickup baseball game.

Mostly though, it's about the lake. In its size and character, it is more like a great sea or ocean. In the middle of summer, when the city is sweltering and humid, Peacock Point is a nearby oasis. There is almost always a cooling breeze that comes in off the lake and after which we named our cottage — "Southwind." On lazy summer afternoons we sit in our wooden chairs, our paperbacks lying unread, our cocktail glasses beaded with sweat, and just gaze out onto the lake, the sunlight dancing across its calm surface like a million tiny, sparkling jewels.

Last July, my ailing father-in-law, who had spent virtually every day of every summer of his boyhood at Peacock Point, made what was to be his last trip to the cottage. With some help, he navigated his walker onto the bank and settled himself into a chair looking out over the lake. It was a typical glorious summer afternoon at Lake Erie, the sun, low in the sky, bathing everything in a soft, honey-golden light. We sat quietly for a while and then my father-in-law said simply, "Pretty nice, isn't it?"

Yup, pretty nice.

Celebrating Two Very Different Lives

February 17, 2006

I went to two very different birthday parties recently. One was for my father-in-law, who turned eighty. The other was for my cousin, who was turning forty. Although their birthdays were only a few days apart, they were people, I first thought, as separated by time, circumstance, and substance as any two birthday celebrants could be.

I was wrong.

My father-in-law, Pete, made it through eight decades of life on December 8. I say "made it" because he would be the first to tell you, he never really thought he'd see eighty. "If I'd known I was going to live this long, I would have taken better care of myself," he often jokes. He is, as he describes himself, a bit "bent, broken, and busted." He's on dialysis three times a week, his right knee is pretty much shot, and he has the beginnings of Alzheimer's, but none of that prevented him from enjoying his birthday.

As a surprise, his youngest daughter, Barb, worked for months putting together a slide show of his life. She tracked down old black-and-white photographs from relatives and friends, carefully scanned them into her computer, and assembled a montage of Pete's life from infancy to eighty. Set to music, it documents a remarkable life, one that was a revelation to the grandchildren in the room, who, for the most part, only knew the man as their kind, white-haired grandpa.

The photos that flashed onto the screen showed another Pete — an athlete of power and skill on the basketball court and the football field, a dashing young man who wooed a beautiful bride, a son who ran his father's manufacturing company, a father to seven children, a harbour commissioner, a friend to many. The photos are filled with laughter, with glasses brimming with whisky — his Irish roots run deep — and, as the slides went on, with more and more faces of those who had passed away.

Pete's wife, Elin, who died suddenly of an aneurysm at forty-six; his best friend, Fred, who went at fifty of a heart attack; his brother and priest, Father Bill — other lifelong friends gone, their smiling faces flashing briefly in the now-quiet room. Then, over the strains of "It's a Wonderful Life," happier times: his marriage to Fred's widow, Fran, and the joining of their large Irish families — thirteen kids in all — more parties, more Christmases, more laughter until the final photo: an exultant Pete, at some long-forgotten event, with his hands raised into the air in a kind of salute to life.

As people wiped away tears and the lights came up, Pete sat motionless, bent over, his head clutched in his hands. A long moment passed. Then, he sat up and said, in a line that perfectly summarizes his nature, "When I see all that, it almost makes me proud to be me."

A few days later, my family is sitting in a brightly lit Chinese restaurant at noon. We are here to celebrate the fortieth birthday of my first cousin Julia Mary. It is, by any measure, an unlikely event. Born premature, weighing about one pound, the doctors gave her little chance to live. She did, but her tiny body had taken a toll: she was brain damaged, she had cerebral palsy, her eyesight was limited, and she suffered terrible and frequent seizures. Again, the doctors told my aunt and uncle she would be lucky to reach her teen years. They were, in one way, right. She was lucky. There were innumerable emergencies, infections, fevers, and seizures, and my aunt and uncle spent what must have amounted to years in doctors' offices, emergency rooms, and clinics. But she lived, and so we find ourselves — aunts, uncles, and cousins — here to celebrate her remarkable four decades of life.

There is no slide show, no list of accomplishments, no companies built, no honours won, no marriages, no children. Just her, much as she has been all her life. Julia is, in most ways, about three years old. She is frozen, in that brief space between infancy and self-consciousness, innocently happy, gentle, and loving. She tears the wrapping paper off her gifts with the abandon of the child she is, ignoring the clothes with a shrug and squealing with uncontrolled glee at the sparkling plastic bracelets and shiny metal watches.

We sing "Happy Birthday" and cut the cake, and my aunt encourages Julia to thank everyone for the gifts. And, somehow, she does. Though she is almost blind and has not been around some of us in months, she steps in close, touches our arms or hands, listens to our voices, and thanks each of us by name.

There are those who are missing. Julia's father, my uncle John, is dead. "Daddy gone to heaven," she says, when she thinks of him this day, and at some point each and every day.

And it is here that the birthdays intersect. They are celebrations of two very different lives — marked by sadness and loss, but most of all, by love. Love, given and received, by a father who has grown old and a daughter who never grew up.

9

Once, Twice, Three Times a Birthday

June 14, 2006

Having three kids of different ages all born on May 29 has led to some strange questions and some hellish parties.

Our son James was born on May 29, 1989.

Our second boy, Matthew, was also born on May 29, but three years later.

And when our daughter, Ella, came, she showed up, yup, that's right, on May 29, 1996. This fact, when it comes up in conversation, always elicits wonder and astonishment.

"Really? That's amazing," people say.

I would agree that it's amazing if I thought I had anything to do with it. But I don't. I have no real clue how it happened. So I usually pause and say, "It's no big deal, really. You just count back nine months and it's my birthday."

There's usually a long moment as people consider this and then, depending on the crowd, it either produces a laugh or a raised eyebrow. It's an old joke, really, so I don't expect much. I use it because my wife and I tend to get some pretty strange questions when we reveal what we sometimes call "the hat trick," this being Canada and all. Some people, before they can help it, say, "How did you do that?"

This question requires some careful consideration. I am pretty sure they really don't want to know exactly how, although I can say we followed the normal procedure as far as I know. They could mean, did we use technology in the process, like artificial insemination, to produce such unerring accuracy? The answer is no, unless you consider lowered lights and playing Frank Sinatra records technological help. I think what they really mean is "Did you plan it that way?" And I would have to say the answer is "Sort of."

Like most people who decide to have children (looking back, you really wonder what you were thinking, don't you?), we thought it might be nice to have a spring baby so that my wife could have the summer off on maternity leave. Of course, actually executing that was not my doing. I have a lot of trouble remembering what month it is, or making it to a dentist appointment, never mind back-calculating conception dates and matching them to menstrual cycles. I mean, come on, most guys get confused with the NHL playoff schedule. No, it was my wife, trusty calendar in hand, who would announce, somewhat officiously, I thought, "Now! Now it's time!" She'd say, "If you don't want to be pushing a baby carriage through snow drifts, we've got to get to work."

Now, some men may find this kind of talk enticing. Perhaps they're accountants or, even better, project managers, but this sort of starter's gun approach was not exactly the kind of invitation I had hoped for. In any case, it worked, more or less, although James, who came five weeks early, wasn't really sticking to the plan.

When we decided to have a second child, I think we just fell into the same pattern and the matching birth date was just pure luck. On Number 3, both fate and modern medicine intervened. My wife could not deliver the usual way because of an obstruction and so the ob-gyn recommended a C-section. We agreed. He leafed through his date book, looked up and said, "How does next Wednesday sound?" We glanced at the calendar, smiled, and said that would be fine. Everything went well, and so we now have three kids with the same birthday.

We thought that was just great until we started trying to organize all the birthdays on one day. The grocery shopping trip that precedes this fateful weekend is bizarre. I end up buying every kind of fried, fatty, fizzy, artificially flavoured food (if you can call it food) known to man. There's usually not a single thing found in nature in my cart. This causes some strange looks at the checkout. After pushing the fourteenth bag of chips through, the cashier looks up and says, "Some birthday party!" and I say, "You don't want to know."

You haven't lived until you've had three kids' birthday parties in a row on a Saturday. Imagine a horde of midget barbarians jacked on gummy bears and root beer. Now multiply by three.

It's a swirling tornado of half-eaten hot dogs, crushed chips, treat bags, yelling, snotty noses, smeared icing, Barney songs, popping balloons, melted ice cream, and birthday cake. And that's before one of them throws up. And they always do. "It's all the excitement," say the parents. Or maybe it's the four hot dogs, two litres of Orange Crush, and half a cake that Johnny ate. Well, ate temporarily.

Then there are the presents. There's nothing quite as scary as a group of toddlers facing a stack of wrapped birthday gifts. It's like a scene from Jaws. Within minutes, the house is knee-deep in torn wrapping paper, toys, and running, wrestling, squealing kids. When they finally leave, the next group arrives. That's like Jaws 2. They're bigger, noisier, and they eat more.

Thankfully, those days are gone. Now that the kids are older, we space out the birthday celebrations so that the parties take up part of the week and the entire weekend. It's a non-stop parade of bowling, movies, video games, fast food, and the ultimate psychological torture for parents — the sleepover. That's when half a dozen thirteen-year-old boys turn your family room into a cross between an all-night 50 Cent concert and an Ultimate Cage Fighting match. Trust me, it's not pretty.

So think of me next May 29, or as we call it, B-Day; I'll be on the front lines.

All things considered, there's no place I'd rather be.

Bon Voyage to a Son and His Childhood

May 28, 2011

We are standing near the departure gates at Pearson International Airport. Our son Matthew is making his way toward the security checkpoint. Tears are streaming down my wife's face as we watch him move closer to the door. He waves back at us. He is smiling.

This all began more than a year ago when Matt, our middle child, announced that he wanted to take some time off and travel in Europe. He and a couple of buddies, Ben and Eric, had a plan to live and work overseas and then do some travelling.

Interesting plan, I said. Where would you like to work? You know, said Matt, in Spain or Italy or France. I pointed out that it might be difficult to secure and hold a job in those countries when none of them actually spoke a single word of Spanish, Italian, or French. Good point, he said, as though the issue has just dawned on him — maybe England would be a better choice.

I was all for the idea, but to tell the truth I had my doubts they would actually organize the excursion. For one, these are guys who can easily sleep until noon, spend the next four hours watching seventeen episodes of the Ricky Gervais Show (which oddly is about three guys sitting around doing nothing but talking), relax a bit, and then take a nap before getting ready to go out for the night.

I mentioned that they would need a few minor items for the trip, like passports, money, and visas — and not the card they use to bankrupt their parents, but real visas that allowed foreigners to live and work abroad.

I told Matt I was happy to help with all this, but that he would have to do the leg work himself. That night I quietly went online and downloaded the forms kindly provided by the British government. It became clear after only six hours trying to read through them that you pretty much needed a Ph.D. in international relations to fill them out.

Luckily, the boys got word about an outfit called SWAP Working Holidays — a students working abroad program. They found out SWAP would help them, but there were a couple of hurdles. One, the British government was not all that interested in having three broke teenagers arriving on their soil equipped with a travel plan based on "tons of drinking and chatting up birds." They demanded $4,000 in a Canadian bank account, new passports, numerous forms filled out, and even a trip to Toronto to be ID'd, fingerprinted, and eye-scanned. At this point I wasn't sure whether they were going on holiday or enlisting in MI5.

But in the next months, Matthew and his pals did what they had to do.

They hatched a plan to land in London and then get jobs and an apartment in the seaside town of Brighton.

But they needed money first, so they got jobs — toiling in restaurant kitchens, clearing tavern tables, working in after-school programs — and they saved their money.

Sure, we helped them out, but it took months for them to build up the required minimum and they did it.

It also took a while to get everything together — the backpacks, money belts, walking boots, travel guides — but in what seemed like weeks, not months, we found ourselves gathered around the dining room table, standing over a cake that read "Bon Voyage!" (which we explained meant "Have a good trip!" in French), watching Matt open envelopes filled with British pounds from relatives and friends. It was that evening, I think, that we realized that Matt, our smiling, chatty, gentle middle child, was really leaving us.

And that's how we found ourselves at the airport on a Tuesday evening nervously watching Matt, and in that moment it seemed only a blink ago that he was a fair-haired baby sliding himself across the kitchen floor on his bum (crawling was too slow for him), his face flushed red, giggling all the way.

So we stood, watching and waving, tears flowing down the faces of all three moms, and I smiled, thinking about teenage boys and leaving home.

For years, on many days, it feels like it can't be soon enough.

And then, suddenly, it's much, much too soon.

A Taste of Something Bitter

January 2, 2008

As I watched my Nonna's pudding come to a slow boil, what bubbled up in me was not nostalgia, but shame.

I was in the kitchen preparing Saturday night's dinner and I had a problem.

Most of the meal was going well. In the oven was *il primo*, the first course, *melanzane parmigiana* — slices of eggplant, tomato sauce, and cheese — slowly filling the kitchen with its earthy aroma. On the stove in front of me was the *secondo*, the main course. I carefully raised the lid of the pot and peeped inside. The *coniglio* — rabbit — was cooking beautifully, simmering in olive oil and white wine and seasoned with rosemary and sage. I prepared a salad of bitter, wine-red radicchio and topped it with chopped fennel, with its crunchy sweetness and hint of licorice.

I was trying to make an authentic Italian dinner. All of these were simple, rustic dishes that I had grown up with, local favourites from the Veneto region in Italy where my father was born and where he spent his youth.

But the problem was dessert, never the highlight of an Italian meal; most dinners end with a strong espresso, a tiny biscotto, and, of course, more wine. So, what to make for dessert?

My mind went back to Saturday afternoons at our home with my father's mother — my Nonna — standing over the stove, wooden spoon in hand, gently stirring the contents of a large steel pot. As a kid I would sit in the kitchen and inhale the almost intoxicating aroma of chocolate and sugar and the slight but unmistakable hint of lemon as she made her specialty, *budino al cioccolato* — homemade chocolate pudding.

Her recipe was in her head, a simple but secret balance of pure cocoa, butter, sugar, flour, and whole milk. It would become a thick, velvety pudding that she would chill and then slice, placing one trembling, treasured slab on each of our plates after dinner.

I decided I would make Nonna's classic pudding.

I called my mother. Although my grandmother had lived with us for decades, she had never divulged the precise recipe. Nonetheless, my mom had a good general guide to making the pudding. My mother is now eighty, and it had been some time since she made it, but she relayed the ingredients to me from a yellowed sheet of paper she had tucked into an old cookbook.

And so I found myself on a Saturday afternoon being propelled back in time, transported by the gentle, hypnotic rhythm of my stirring and the rich, deep scent of cocoa that filled the room. But as I watched the pudding come to a slow boil, what bubbled up in me was not nostalgia, but shame. I had not been particularly good to my Nonna. She was in many ways a difficult woman: nervous, self-centred, mildly hypochondriac, and not above playing favourites with her grandchildren.

She made it clear I was not her favourite and I responded childishly by antagonizing her. I would mimic her heavily accented English and mock her shuffling walk. I would talk back to her and make jokes about her in front of my friends.

She was not easily angered, but when she had finally had enough, she would look at me disapprovingly, shaking her head and waving her hand back and forth, and say, "*Cattivo ragazzo*" ("bad boy"). I would mirror her actions and repeat her criticisms in a whiny, mocking tone.

I would do all this despite the wrath of my father, who when informed of my behaviour would demand that I respect my grandmother. I didn't.

A few years later, when I was old enough to know better, I could not find the moment or the words to apologize. When perhaps I was finally ready, my grandmother had slipped out of reach, her mind stolen by dementia. And now that my mother is as old as my Nonna was then, I can only look back at my antics with a queasy mixture of regret and shame.

I made the pudding, and it came out near perfect.

I saved two slices, and on Sunday drove them up to my parents. My father tasted the pudding and pronounced it "beautiful, like your Nonna's."

Who can say how we are linked, how our past dictates our present, what unknowable mix of genes and experiences shapes us? I thought of my father as a child eating the pudding his mother had made for him, of me as a kid sneaking an extra piece and now making the same dessert for my children and my parents, our roles at once parallel and oddly reversed.

I felt all of this at once, my connection across blood and time to the past, a past rich and sweet, and somewhere in that heady mix a vague hint, a taste of something bitter.

12

Two Gallons of Losing My Mind, Please

July 9, 2011

We decided to paint the cottage this summer.

I know, on the face of it, that sounds like a pretty simple idea.

Buy paint. Buy brushes. Paint inside of cottage.

It involves absolutely no real technical skill and no required contact with machinery that has moving parts. In other words, the perfect job for me. And because there would be no one there to oversee the project, it was also perfect for unlimited coffee breaks and occasional naps (to allow things to dry, of course.)

But all of that is predicated on the assumption that you actually buy the paint. And that is based on the idea that you agree on the colour of the paint. This has turned out to be only slightly more complicated than manned space flight or making Stephen Harper laugh.

Part of the problem is the simple fact of multiple owners. This was not an issue when we rebuilt the old cottage with my wife's sister Brenda and her husband, Woody. It was no problem because what I knew about building a new cottage could be fit onto a Smartie with room left for a map of the world. So, wisely, I just said, "Woody, you build it."

To maintain some sense of masculinity, though, I would occasionally interject comments (in a deep voice) like, "Well, I INSIST on walls or I'm not paying," or, if I'd been drinking, "Oh, listen to you, Mr.

Paul Benedetti

Sixteen-Inch-Joists this and Mr. Poured-Concrete-Footings that. But how would you do in an arm wrestle, eh? I ask you that!"

After this, my wife would walk me down the hall and put me to sleep and construction would resume.

But the problem with painting is that everyone, and I mean everyone — kids, grandparents, pets — has an opinion about colour. Not surprisingly, to preserve sanity and marriages, the cottage is currently what I like to call "Compromise Beige," the universal paint shade of anyone who has given up on the Colour War. Of course, this colour is NEVER actually called beige. Oh no, it's got names like (and I am not making these up) Barnacle or Thatch or Louisbourg or Pelee Island or Secord or Fieldstone or Galloway. How do they come up with this stuff anyway? Are there guys sitting around in a room all day wearing black turtlenecks and sipping cappuccinos staring at a square of beige paint yelling out random words?

Anyway, the first thing we wanted, after ten years of beige, was to, as my wife kept saying, "shake things up a bit." And by this she means painting the walls a colour that would keep a blind man up at night. Of course, this was better than the fateful words that would change everything: "Paul, don't you think babies are soooooo cute?" Sorry, I mean, "Maybe we should hire a designer."

Oddly, considering the cost of raising a child today — with their ridiculous demands for things like iPods and, you know, food — it's the second sentence that is the more costly. So, I quietly suggested this was not a good idea. I think my exact words were, "Oh, for God's sake, it's a cottage on Lake Erie! Who are we impressing? Manny, the guy who comes to pump out the septic tank?" Or words to that effect.

Anyway, we agreed to choose the colours on our own, a process that has now gone on longer than the painting of the Sistine Chapel.

We have considered colours with names like (and again, I am not making this up, though I wish I were) Girls Rule, Meet for Drinks, and Skinny Jeans.

Try going into Home Depot and asking the big guy in the paint department to mix you up a can of Angel Wings or Dreams Come True.

I dare you.

So, after much wrangling, several threats to "call in the designer," and at least one arm wrestle (Brenda beat me), we decided on a colour called Clam Shell for the walls and one called Elephant for the doors. These are, to the naked, non-professional person's eye, Grey and Slightly Darker Grey. In fact, now that I look at the walls, the colour is a lot like, well, beige.

I like it.

13

At the End, a Week-Long Celebration of Life

March 22, 2008

About a year ago, for one week, each and every day, I watched my father-in-law die.

It was not, as you might expect, a sombre vigil. In fact, it turned out to be quite a party. Pete, as he was affectionately called, even by his children, had the rare opportunity to preside over his own wake. Irish by heritage and Irish in character, he never missed a chance to have fun, and this would be no exception. His last week on Earth was filled with stories and songs, tears and laughs, and more than a few glasses of his favourite drink — rye and water — and next to the birth of my children, it was the most beautiful thing I have ever seen.

Pete was eighty-one and had been on dialysis for almost a decade. Though he was an imposing man — six foot three and 230 pounds with a full head of silver-grey hair — the nurses at the dialysis unit loved him for his gentle and gracious nature.

Christmas that year was difficult for Pete, and by January it was clear to everyone that he was failing. He was in pain, more fatigued and frequently more confused. In his life he had occasionally characterized an older person as someone "who didn't know if it was Tuesday or next week." That, ironically, now applied to him, and he knew it.

His children, all six daughters and a son, convened to figure out how to best help their father. For days they talked late into the night, but their deliberations were pre-empted when internal bleeding landed Pete in hospital. His kidneys had completely shut down, and more importantly tests confirmed his body was riddled with cancer. A young, earnest doctor looked him in the eye and told him what he likely already knew.

"You mean I'm at the end of the road?" asked Pete. Yes, said the doctor. Pete looked at him and then deadpanned, "Are you sure you know what you're talking about?" Slightly flustered, the doctor assured him that he did. "Okay," said Pete. "Thanks."

He did not express anger or fear then or in the days that followed. He had his final dialysis treatment, and on a snowy Sunday morning he went home.

There, his wife, his children, and his six stepchildren (he had remarried after his first wife died suddenly at age forty-six) gathered around him. And the party began. Seated in his oversized chair in the living room, Pete held court. Relatives and friends poured in. At cocktail hour, food was served and the drinks flowed. Somehow, inexplicably, Pete's confusion lifted. Names came back. Stories poured out. He was faster, funnier, more present than he had been in years. He was, perhaps for the first time in a long time, happy. Really happy.

After several days, he grew tired and could no longer get out of bed, but the party didn't end, it just shifted to his room. His wife and children sat in bed with him, did crossword puzzles, watched game shows, said some prayers, and held his hand.

Pete grew weaker, and by Saturday night, almost a week after he had come home, he grew silent.

That evening, his wife lay down beside him and his children filled his small bedroom. There, in the darkened room, they began to sing his favourite songs — ditties, hymns, and fragments of show tunes.

Then we played the slide show from his eightieth birthday party. He silently watched the photos that documented his full, rich life flicker by on the computer screen, and when the music ended and the room fell silent, Pete smiled and weakly made the motion of clapping. I think all of us knew this would be the last good day, and every person wished him good night and said the words he had so often and so freely said to them: "I love you."

And with that, Pete went to sleep. A few hours later, he took a final breath and gently left this life. Although it is impossible to know, I like to think he did it with a smile.

14

Being There

June 14, 2008

When I heard my wife's voice on the phone I knew something was wrong.

She was calling to let me know that her stepsister Margy had just come out of a meeting with her oncologist. Not long ago, Margy had bravely decided to try another course of medication for her cancer. She had recently completed two weeks of a difficult, sometimes painful treatment, using a drug that was on the cutting edge but that had a low chance of success. Not the best odds, but the best she had.

My wife related the story. The doctor started by asking Margy how she thought the treatment had gone. Margy paused and said, "I don't think it worked."

The doctor, with the scan results in front of him on the desk, looked straight at her and said, "You're right."

There was a pause on the line.

"That's too bad," I said, realizing even as I said it, how inadequate a response it was. "Now what?" I asked my wife.

"Well, Margy would like us all to get together for dinner tonight."

For a minute I didn't know what to say. Get together? For dinner? I am embarrassed to admit that my first impulse was to say no. I didn't want to go, didn't want to deal with the situation. What would we say? What would it be like? I wasn't even sure it was a good idea. But my wife, from whom I have learned a great deal in these matters, was sure.

"What would we do exactly?" I said.

"Be there."

And so we gathered together, sisters, stepsisters, spouses, Margy's mother. On the stove was a tall pot filled to the brim with tomato sauce, bubbling away, filling the kitchen with a familiar, comforting aroma. Thank God somebody always makes tomato sauce. As wine bottles were opened, the sounds of corks being pulled out punctuated the early awkward silences. But before long we were milling around the kitchen, talking, setting the table, catching up.

Moments later, Margy and her husband, Dave, arrived. Margy looked well. After the meeting with the doctor, she and her sisters had decided to go for a long lunch. Margy felt like french fries, so that's what they ordered. Afterward, fatigued both mentally and physically, she had gone home, had a nap, and now she was here.

We talked about everything — jobs, kids, dogs, the hockey playoffs — and nothing. After a while, Margy talked about her illness. She seemed calm and clear about it and talked about moving forward. Through the evening, there were laughs and sometimes tears. And if you wandered out of the kitchen, you might find people in the living room speaking in hushed tones or standing on the deck quietly wiping tears from their eyes.

Even now I'm not sure what kind of evening it was, but I'm sure about one thing. I'm glad I went. I'm glad we were there. Perhaps we accomplished nothing much more than that — being together with Margy on a night when no one wanted to be alone. When being surrounded by the people you grew up with, the people you love, is what you need to get through the night. And it turned out to be, in some odd way, a good night.

We often leave people alone in their lowest moments. "Don't bother them now," people say. "They need their privacy." I know, because I have said those words. And I have come to know that what we're really saying is, "I don't know what to do," or more honestly, "I'm afraid." But in the last few years, like most people my age, I have watched people close to me lose a parent or a sibling, have a child fall gravely ill, or get cancer news that is bad. And what I have come to know is those are the moments when they need you the most.

In the end, I suppose, nobody really knows what the future holds and each of us must face things on our own — make our own peace with the hand we're dealt. But in the meantime, you can eat pasta together, you can drink wine together, you can talk about everything, you can talk about nothing, or not talk at all. But, most importantly, you can do the one thing that really matters: be there.

15

"But What's Going to Happen to My Stuff?"

November 29, 2008

There's nothing quite like the shock of seeing a FOR SALE sign on your parent's house.

At first, you figure it's a trick of the eye; the sign is on the next lawn over. Then, as you get closer, you realize no, it's really there.

Then you hope that perhaps you just weren't paying attention and an election is actually on and the guy running is named Re Max. But, you decide, you'd have to be some dumb politician to actually announce that you were "for sale." Though, come to think of it, that would speed the whole "governing" thing up considerably.

Finally, you accept it: the house … hell, your house … is up for sale. And you're peeved.

You know, you leave for one minute — okay, maybe thirty years — and bam! Your mom sells your room on you.

This raises several key issues.

One, you no longer have a safety net if your wife finally kicks you out for:

    a. excessive snoring;
    b. excessive snoring coupled with extreme "beer smell"; or
    c. excessive snoring while she's talking to you.

You could really be in trouble. In the good old days, when you had a "home" to go to, this idle threat was meaningless. But now, the whole surgery-to-get-your-epiglottis-cut-off is starting to look pretty good.

The next issue is Your Stuff. What's going to happen to it? You suddenly remember that when you moved out you took only the absolute necessities needed to set up your own apartment: Beer. A stereo. Some snacks.

The rest you left behind. You promised to come back in a week and clean up, but a few things came up and you missed a few decades. Now, your mom, sensing your fragile emotional state, calls and says, "Hey, can you get your junk out of here? I'm trying to move!"

So you go over and start. In the basement you find your weights — a bench press, the bar, and the old Weider plastic plates you bought when you thought girls were interested in big arms. (Soon, you realized many were more interested in other things being big — like investment portfolios). For old times' sake, you lie down and try to crank out a few reps on the bench press. Later, after the firemen and paramedics leave, you explain that you felt you were still in "pretty good shape" even though you had taken a short thirty-year break from weightlifting.

After a rest and a nice sandwich your mom made (gee, it's great to be home), you tackle the other stuff. Immediately you find every university textbook you ever had — many of them strangely unread and in perfect condition. Next, you discover a box full of assignments and report cards from school and you smile, remembering the great old days and how well you did — not like these darn kids today with their iPods and their online games.

Then you read some of the comments: "Paul would do better if he applied himself. Seems inordinately interested in his hair" and "Paul participates in class. Too bad he is something of a jackass."

These you put through the shredder in case your kids ever got a hold of them and you blew your already tenuous role as The Guy Yelling at Them to Get Their Homework Done.

You save a couple of postcards, some comic books, a 1972 copy of Playboy (hey, that's a cultural artifact — you know, like Ed Broadbent), and a letter or two. You destroy a few pictures — "What stripper? There was no stripper at my bachelor party!" — and you pack the rest in a box.

You're feeling a bit down until your mom reminds you that there's a nice second bedroom in the new place for any of the kids "who want to sleep over."

She means the grandchildren, but who cares?

There's no place like home — but a spare room at the retirement village will do in a pinch.

16

Dad's Christmas Was About Family,
Not Turkey

December 27, 2008

My dad was not that big on Christmas.

For one thing, like a lot of Italians, he took a dim view of turkey. He had trouble getting excited about a meal built around what he thought was essentially a giant chicken that produced a pile of dried-out, stringy, tasteless white meat.

He thought mashed up squash was baby food and that cooked cranberries might be okay on ice cream, but only crazy people (a.k.a. the English) ate it with dinner. Ditto for candied yams, and any salad with tangerines in it. (Are these people completely crazy?) He thought Brussels sprouts should remain in Brussels and he had mixed feelings about stuffing, mainly because he was dubious about anything you had to shovel out of a turkey's bum onto your plate.

He did not hide his lack of enthusiasm for the traditional Christmas dinner, but he ate it the way the citizens of Italy pay taxes — sparingly and grudgingly.

He was also not all that big on the whole Christmas "thing," in fact. I think some of that was cultural. A lot of Christmas traditions in Canada come from Germany. I doubt little Italian kids were thrilled about the idea of an overweight, red-faced German guy named Klaus crashing into their house in the dead of night — with or without presents. And most Italians would think a guy in a baggy, ill-fitting red suit needed a new tailor, not milk and cookies.

He also considered other German-based seasonal customs, such as dragging a live tree into your living room and dressing it up like Liberace, to be a bit odd. Similarly, he thought mulling wine was for mullet heads. What kind of idiot ruins perfectly good red wine by heating it up and adding slices of fruit to it?

So, we did all this stuff (okay, we didn't mull wine — there were limits), but my father was kind of half-hearted about most of it.

Unfortunately for us, he brought the same lack of enthusiasm to gift-buying. Natale in Italy was mostly a religious celebration that did not, apparently, include typing out a long list of preferred presents and handing it to your parents. My dad liked giving gifts — but not on demand. He bristled at the idea of being treated like some kind of human Sears catalogue. So, he really did stomp around saying, "It's Christmas around here every day," and he was never very keen on the gifts he got. "If I wanted a pair of slippers, I'd have bought myself a pair," he'd say, and you could almost hear the added "and probably not these." (Later, we all gave up trying to buy him real gifts and he seemed pretty happy unwrapping one bottle of cognac after another.) But, despite all the grumbling, he always broke down and made sure there were gifts for everyone under the tree, though the only thing he ever wrapped in his life were fish bones to throw in the garbage.

What he really liked was getting everyone together, especially the little kids. He loved their barely controlled excitement and enjoyed their squeals and laughter as they tore into the gifts. Later, he'd call them over one by one and slip some money to them, and every year, in what had become an annual tradition, he'd ask one of them to "Smell this pie. I think something's wrong with it" and smoosh the meringue into their face to the delight of the other kids.

For the first time, my dad wasn't here for Christmas this year. He died this past summer. His absence left a hole in Christmas that no food or gifts could fill. We missed him. But I don't think he would miss the turkey.

17

Lessons on Living

January 24, 2009

When five women came up to the podium with pink boas around their necks and diamond tiaras equipped with red flashing lights on their heads, you knew it was not going to be a regular funeral reception.

They were, they explained, The Secret Society of Queens on a King — five women who met each Wednesday on a king-sized bed to sit and talk and drink and laugh, always laugh, with their sick friend, Margy — the Sixth Queen.

There, Margy, weakened by the renal-cell carcinoma that had been spreading through her body for the past two years, held court. The women — sisters, neighbours, and childhood friends — discussed symptoms, talked about kids and husbands, invented a new cocktail (one part Grand Marnier, one part Kahlua and one part Baileys), and welcomed whoever happened to drop in.

And they did drop in. Margy, my wife's stepsister, wanted it that way. She had, after her diagnosis of cancer, chosen a rare path. Rather than retreat into her illness and disengage from the world, she embarked upon a mission to get well, but also to live life with the knowledge that she might not. Navigating such a course requires a delicate balancing of two of life's essential skills — accepting what is and hoping for what might be. Margy did this with remarkable grace and an unusual candour.

At the funeral reception last week, her friend JoAnne expressed it well, saying, "And throughout it all, despite her deteriorating condition and many discouraging setbacks, Margy remained the same — positive, humorous, determined, courageous, and unwaveringly honest."

It was that honesty that gave her the strength to travel, catching up on some special trips she and her husband, Dave, had, in the whirlwind of raising three kid, never quite found the time to take. In between debilitating chemotherapy sessions, there was a family Caribbean cruise, a magical trip to Paris and Greece with friends, and a final Christmas holiday in the Dominican Republic. It was that honesty that allowed her — when it became clear to the doctors and to her — to tell people that her cancer was incurable and that she had perhaps another year or so, and that she was going to live each day as best she could.

Make no mistake, at only fifty-one years of age, Margy hated the idea of dying, hated most the very thought of leaving her children and her husband. But because she was so open about this, there was no pretense with her family and friends, and knowing the truth made every day, even the bad ones, important. Margy surrounded herself with people and as they tried to comfort and help her, something remarkable happened.

It soon became clear to the people around her that, as much as they were helping her, she was helping them. She brought childhood friends back in touch, put cancer survivors in the same room, drew people, both the strong and the wounded, together, and pulled family closer in a way that may have been more thought-out and thoughtful than anyone imagined. Again, it was her friend JoAnne who expressed this revelation. "In retrospect, it is clear that from the moment of her first diagnosis, Margy had a plan. She set out to show us and teach us so many things."

And so, though they must have been in unspeakable pain, Margy's three children neither complained nor raged when they addressed the funeral guests. Instead, they did something wonderful. They thanked everyone for their kindness and generosity, and then they thanked their mother, for the gifts she gave them in her life and her death.

And when her husband of twenty-five years, Dave, came up to the podium, he gave words to a feeling, an idea, that grew as each person spoke of Margy's journey until it seemed to fill the room. That her life and death had awakened in him "an undeniable belief in the strength of the human spirit, of love and compassion, that the world is indeed full of angels."

18

"What Do You Have in Mind, Dear?"

February 21, 2009

A few days ago, I found my wife sitting in the living room just looking around. This is a very bad sign. It could mean a number of things, including:

1. She's suddenly thinking about the words her father said as he walked her up the aisle on our wedding day. "You don't have to marry this guy. It's not too late to back out."
2. She inadvertently opened our RRSP statement and has plunged into a coma-like state of shock.
3. She's thinking about redecorating.

"I'm thinking we should do something with this room," she says. I never know what this means. It seems to me that most rooms are "doing just fine" most of the time and that any human intervention on this front is crazy. What do we want to do with the room? Take it out to dance lessons? Introduce it to another room on the street?

Naturally, I keep these ideas to myself so that I can enjoy a few more years outside of a mental institution.

Unable to control myself, I say the words that can very easily lead to:

a. Financial insolvency

b. Divorce

c. Filling out applications to get on *Extreme Makeover: Home Edition*

The words are, "What do you have in mind, dear?"

She explains that several friends who came over felt the room was "too low." To me, the room appears to be comfortably at sea level, but it turns out that our living room is "bottom heavy" and that we need to "move the eye upward to make the room lighter and more spacious." I translate this into, "I'm an interior decorator and I say crazy things to people."

As well, it appears that our colours are dull and earthy and need a "splash of red."

I know, from leafing through home decorating magazines when no one is looking, that the editors of these journals alternate monthly between two ideas: "Neutrals are back! Make your home a sea of tranquility and style with white, beige, and grey." (Only they call these colours ivory, café, and cement.) OR "Dull is out! Energize your home with daring COLOUR! (The word *colour* has the letters in a rainbow of vibrant hues.) This keeps readers confused and painters in business.

I assume the room advice means we have to re-hang some pictures so that they are in decorating terms "higher," and buy four bright-red throw pillows. I am wrong.

It turns out we have to have all our furniture re-covered. This shocks me. We bought our living room couch a mere two decades ago, and except for the worn out bum spots on the cushions and the delightful pattern of stains from the baby barf of three kids, they look perfectly fine to me. I argued vigorously and intelligently and made several excellent points while I was carrying the furniture out to the upholstery shop truck.

When the furniture returned, it looked great.

Luckily, I had managed to convince my wife that having bright red furniture, though fun for Christmas and Valentine's Day, might be too visually overwhelming or as I put it, "insane."

Unfortunately, the newly re-covered furniture made it even more obvious that our room lacked "flow" and was "blocked up," said the decorating friends. I suggested we give the living room more fibre. Apparently, this is not considered funny in home decorating circles and I was sent to the kitchen.

To improve the flow, we had to move all the furniture in the room — including a piano that weighs just a bit less than Cape Breton — across the room several times and back again. When we were done, the room felt "higher," but that might have been because I was viewing it from the floor, where I was lying in a back spasm.

Oh, and the splash of red? Easy — new pillows, candles, and this month's bank statement.

19

What, Me Forgetful?

March 21, 2009

Last Friday, I went over to my neighbour Dave's house to borrow a piece of garlic. While I was there I also decided to borrow some gin, which Dave conveniently provided in a large crystal glass. I borrowed some ice, too.

I had not even been there an hour when the inevitable phone call came.

"It's your wife," said Dave.

"Hello," I said, hoping she might not recognize my voice.

"What are you doing over there? I hear reggae music."

I explained that while Dave was looking for the garlic, an impromptu limbo party had broken out.

"Well, you better come home right now. The police have called for you."

I carried my borrowed gin home. Unfortunately, I had forgotten the garlic or whatever it was I went over there for.

The police say you stole gas, said my wife, not laughing.

"That's absurd," I said. "Now that the price has come down, I stopped stealing gas months ago."

"Funny. The officer said someone pumped a tankful of gas and then drove away without paying."

I told her that was impossible. I always use my credit card to buy gas because we are trying to build up our travel points.

It seems to be working. Now, after using the card for several years, I have checked the website and discovered I have enough points for a bus trip to Ingersoll. One way. Or a very nice stapler.

Anyway, I phoned Hamilton Police Service, and a polite officer answered and told me he was following up on a theft report.

"Yes, yes, "I said. "Look officer, there must be some mistake. It's impossible. I don't steal. Anything. Well, I might pop the odd grape when I'm at Fortinos, but really that's not stealing is it? I mean, come on. I've seen women there pretty much eat a whole fruit salad while they walk through produce."

At this point, I couldn't help but notice my wife giving me the universal sign for "shut up."

"Actually, that is stealing," said the officer, "but perhaps we can stick to the matter at hand. I know it's dinnertime, and I don't want to bother you at home."

"Yes, I'm right in the middle of cooking some martinis," I said. "I think there's been some kind of mistake."

"Do you drive a silver Toyota?"

"Yes."

"Did you buy gas tonight at a Sunoco station?"

"Yes."

"About 6:45 p.m.?"

"Yes."

"Are you an aging Italian man with a large nose and a strangely awkward walking style?"

"Well, I don't know if that's really accurate."

"Just kidding. Your wife actually told me to say that. But the rest is correct?"

"Yes."

"Well, either you or Ralph Macchio pumped $33 worth of gas into your tank and forgot to pay. We suggest you return to the station and clear things up."

I thanked him and hung up the phone. It appears, I said, that against all odds, I may have somehow forgotten to pay for the gas.

It was at this point my wife, in that gentle way she has, reminded me that I had in the past:

1. left our daughter at school until the janitor called saying he was locking up for the night;
2. left the car running for three hours after I parked it at the Simcoe fall fair (At the time, I explained that I had done this on purpose to "clear out the engine grime."); and
3. forgotten to load our suitcases for an anniversary weekend in Niagara-on-the-Lake, forcing us to dine at local restaurants in our bathrobes. (We told people we were Swedish.)

I went to the gas station, apologized, and paid my bill. On the way home I stopped at Dave's to borrow something, but I can't remember what.

20

The Lawn and Short of It: I Don't Care

April 18, 2009

On the weekend a young man came to the door and asked if I would be interested in environmental air-rationing. I had several key questions.

1. Would saying yes mean that I would pay a fixed rate for natural gas for the next five years? (Or the opposite? I'm never sure.)
2. Would I have to run, walk, skip, or dance the mambo for many hours, and get reluctant friends and relatives to sponsor me?
3. If I said yes, would I receive a magazine of any kind or a T-shirt that said, "I'm helping to save the world. What are you doing, you fat-cat, capitalist bastard?"

As I was thinking about this, apparently several minutes passed and I may have drooled a little on my shirt. "Sir, are you okay?" he said.

I recovered quickly and said cleverly, "I might say yes, but I'm not sure what air-rationing is."

"I said 'aeration,' not 'air-ration,'" he said helpfully.

We went back and forth like this for five or ten minutes. Finally, he said, "Look, I drive a machine over your lawn and it punches out little plugs of dirt that look like about a hundred cocker spaniels just visited your grass."

I had seen this done on the properties of other people who cared about their lawns. "That's nothing I couldn't do myself with a melon baller and about forty or fifty spare hours."

"That's right, but I can do it for you right now. Front and back is fifty bucks. For front only, it's thirty — on special today."

"It's kind of a small front lawn," I said. "How does twenty-five dollars sound?"

"Does this look like a vending stall in Istanbul?" he said. "What are you, a weasel? I'm just a student trying to make enough money to pay for my tuition, my books, and the odd night of binge drinking."

We settled on thirty-five dollars, the extra five to avoid the "optional ventilation" of my porch.

This first step in lawn maintenance was a big deal for me. If you can imagine the way a perfectly groomed golf green looks in early summer, my lawn looks nothing like that. It's mostly a dried up, patchy mess, if I really take care of it.

By early summer each year my neighbour, who is not Dave (actually, it is Dave, but I don't want to appear to pick on him as he often provides free before-dinner drinks) comes over to talk about my grass. "Do you realize that your lawn is covered in dandelions? What are you going to do about it?"

I never know how to answer this. I could pull them all out and make a nice dandelion salad, but if you saw the number of dogs that "visit" our front lawn, you'd rethink that idea. I could actually do some lawn work, or I could say I hear the phone ringing, go into the house, and just never come back out.

Instead, I said, "What's wrong with a few dandelions? Their bright yellow flowers are in many cultures a welcome harbinger of summer."

"You're insane," he said. "Dandelions are one of nature's most dangerous and prolific producers of noxious vegetation. That cute puffball you seem to enjoy so much is actually the A-bomb of weeds, and the prevailing southerly wind in this area means that very soon millions and millions of weed spores will BLOW DOWN THE STREET ONTO MY LAWN!"

At this point, Dave was screaming, so I asked him to lie on the couch and I put a cold washcloth on his forehead. Later, after a promise to get rid of the weeds and several gin and tonics, he seemed better and was able to go home.

The aeration worked out. I don't know about the grass, but I think the weeds are going to love it.

21

Looking Mortality in the Eye

The first death was like this. We were at the breakfast table going through the newspapers when my wife said, "This is my friend." All the blood had drained from her face and her eyes filled with tears. "Born: 1961. This is Monique. She's dead."

A close high-school friend, Monique had been killed in a car accident near Cranbrook, B.C. Driving along a mountain highway with her partner on a clear April Sunday morning, they came over the crest of a hill and slammed into the back of a slow-moving transport truck. They were both killed instantly. She was forty-seven.

A few days later, the phone rang. A close friend's sister was vacationing in Cancun with her husband and their young daughter. On the last day of the vacation, they were sitting by the pool and her husband, John, said: "I think I'll go for one more swim in the ocean." He never came back. Perhaps he was knocked over by a wave or pulled in by the undertow, no one is sure. But, only minutes after he left, people found his body floating in the shallow water. He was forty-four.

Then, five days later, on a sunny spring Saturday morning, the phone rang. My wife's first cousin Theresa and her husband, Daryl, were on the 401, heading to Detroit to watch their son — one of their five children — compete in a university track meet. They had just stopped for coffee and Theresa offered to drive. "It's okay," said Daryl. "Have your breakfast. We'll switch at Chatham." In the warm sunshine, along that straight, flat stretch of road, in the smallest moment, the car drifted to the shoulder, the noise of the tires startling Theresa. "Daryl," she said, and then they were rolling, over once and then again, the crumpled car coming to rest in the oncoming lanes. Theresa dialed 911 and people rushed to the wreckage, but she knew it didn't really matter. Daryl, her high school sweetheart, her husband for twenty-five years, his head resting gently in her lap, wasn't breathing. Later, Theresa would say she knew he was dead on the first roll, his head hitting the side of the car as they pitched over. He was forty-eight.

In the lineup at the funeral home in Thorold, a line that snaked through every room and out the door and down the driveway to the street, hundreds and hundreds of people waited, sometimes for hours, until the funeral home people had to shake their heads and close the doors and say please come back later. In that lineup, Nancy, one of Theresa's nine siblings, found us and we asked how Theresa was. And Nancy, her eyes brimming with tears, said: "She's okay, but her heart is broken."

The next day at the funeral, thousands of people filled the church, over-flowing into the aisles and down into the basement, and thousands more filled the nearby high school where Daryl taught phys ed and coached dozens of teams and touched the lives of thousands of kids and their families, and it seemed as though the whole town of Thorold had come out in their shock and grief to pay him tribute. Later, someone said Daryl would have been bewildered by the event. They could hear him saying, "Heck, I'm just a gym teacher."

In the days that follow, I think about Monique and John and Daryl and I am shaken, reminded that we are fragile things and that our hold on life is gossamer thin. How do you live when you can, in the briefest moment, disappear?

And so one morning I find myself rooting through a box for an old clipping, a story by John Diamond, an English writer who in 2001, at the age of forty-seven and dying from cancer, was asked to write about the meaning of life or, as the editor put it, "What the hell is the point of it all?"

Diamond's answer was, in the end, deceptively simple. The point of life is to live it. Fully. Abundantly. Happily. He wrote, "This is the point of it all. You aren't happy? Yes you are: this, here, now, is what happiness is. Enjoy it."

Two months later, he was dead.

22

The Non-Golfer Cooks in Myrtle Beach

May 16, 2009

This year the Boys' Trip was to Myrtle Beach. I really wanted to go because, of late, what used to be an annual trip has turned into a once-every-two-or-three-years trip.

There are several reasons for this:

1. People have very busy lives. Translation: "If you think you're going on a boys' trip when we haven't had a weekend getaway in five years, you're out of your mind."
2. Pressures from the global recession. Translation: same as above.
3. It's now taking about two years for us to recover from each trip.

This year's trip, organized by my friend John, was billed as "three days of golf, sunshine, and unlimited wet towel-snapping." My problem is I don't golf. It's not that I'm a bad golfer, it's that I've never played a round in my life.

I did go out to a driving range once. There, after a few swings — several of which actually resulted in contact with the ball — EMS was called by my fellow golfers, who, for some odd reason, thought I was having a seizure.

Now, my association with golf is limited to going to parties and saying, "How about that Tiger Woods, eh?"

Anyway, my wife was extremely understanding, and after several days of non-stop pleading and a couple of notarized documents legally binding me or any "future husband" to several "excursions to Niagara-on-the-Lake to include but not be limited to: shopping, spa treatments, and egregiously expensive dinners," I found myself on my way to Myrtle Beach.

We flew out of Buffalo and the first thing I noticed was that about several hundred other American guys had stolen our idea. You did not have to be with CSIS to pick them out. Every guy over forty was wearing the identical outfit: khaki-coloured chinos, penny loafers, a blue button-down shirt, and a can of Budweiser. The wilder ones — possibly Democrats — wore no socks.

Several Budweisers later, I also had no socks, and we arrived in Myrtle Beach. For some reason — possibly stupidity — I had assumed a place with a name like Myrtle Beach was a quaint seaside town, something like Port Dover but with more automatic weapons.

On the drive into town, I realized that, like everything in America, it was GIGANTIC.

As well, it became clear that the city's civic fathers had carefully overseen its growth to ensure that any human being who tried to live there without a car would be dead within a few days.

Myrtle Beach is really just a stretch of highway flanked on both sides by an endless stream of beachwear stores, mini-golf parks filled with giant plastic dinosaurs and pirate ships (well, those are the tasteful ones), car washes, pawn shops, and innumerable all-you-can-eat seafood buffets with names like O'Malley's or O'Casey's, which is odd because though they are fine people, the Irish are not renowned for their culinary expertise with fish or anything else unless you consider Guinness a food, which they clearly do.

Judging by the sheer number of such eateries, the idea of leaving mounds of fresh seafood out on counters all day in a place where the temperature hovers in the eighties (a food practice that Canadian nutrition experts term "pants-on-head-crazy") is appealing to many Americans. Our group, on the other hand, preferred to live, so I found my role for the weekend.

I was the cook.

That's right, while the other guys were out shooting eighteen, my friend Lou and I drove from one GIANT BOX STORE to another, filling shopping carts with everything we'd need for the weekend — steaks, beer, coffee, horseradish, beer, and beer.

I prepped, I cooked, and everyone helped clean up.

It was pretty much just like home, except for the help-cleaning-up part.

23

The Confusing Gap Between
What They Say and What I Hear

May 30, 2009

I'm not sure what people are saying to me anymore.

Not all the time, of course. I understand simple commands. Well, mostly. Sometimes when I'm at the drug store and the clerk says "Opnumcurd?" it takes me a minute to realize she's not speaking Urdu.

Things got a bit worse last weekend. My wife and I were at a lovely party at our neighbour's home. The house filled with people, everyone grabbed a drink, the music was playing, and soon the room was humming with conversations and laughter. I was in the crowded living room trying to talk to a nice couple who mentioned their vacation. How was it? I said. Then he said something about a D.U.I. and "nailing a cat with a van." I nodded seriously, but they seemed oddly casual about it all. Then he said a few more things I couldn't hear and then something about "deluded bitches." His wife smiled and said, "Oh, yes, and we ate nude."

I'm a pretty open guy, but I really had nothing for that, so I excused myself and went into the kitchen. My wife was there and I told her who I had just been talking to. "Wow," I said, "they sure have some interesting ideas about travel."

"Yes," she said. "I'm so jealous. The B.V.I., sailing a catamaran! Secluded beaches. Great food. We should do that one day."

Yes, yes, I said, glad I had not asked more about the nude dining, which had actually piqued my interest.

I wandered into the family room. The music was louder there, but there were fewer people. I saw Phil, the host. He looked good, maybe a little flustered from all the party preparations. "How are you?" I yelled.

"Oh, okay," he said. "Did you hear what happened?"

Then he told me — how to put this as delicately as possible — that he had damaged an important body part, below the waist, last weekend. "It was dark. You know how it goes. A few inches either way can make all the difference."

"God, that's terrible," I said.

"Yeah, I almost lost my whole 'lower unit,'" he said. "Unbelievable."

"Is it, you know, going to be okay?" I muttered.

"They say they can fix it. It could take a while before they get to it. It's all right though. Lately, I only take it out on the weekend anyway."

"Yeah, I know what that's like," I said, trying to go along with things. "I mean, how are you about it all?"

"Oh, you know, a bit embarrassed. You never think it'll happen to you. My wife's not too happy."

"Yes, I can see that," I said awkwardly. "I think I need a drink."

In the kitchen, I came face to face with Phil's wife. I wasn't sure what to say. She seemed awfully perky considering the circumstances. "I'm ... I'm, you know, sorry to hear about what happened to Phil," I said.

"Oh yes. Can you believe it?" she said. "He pretty much wrecked his prop. It was foggy and he hit a shoal. Thank goodness he didn't sink the boat!"

I thought I was alone with this problem, but recently I received an email from a friend. He wrote that he had taken his mom out for dinner last week. She was recounting the events of her day and my friend admitted that his attention wandered over to the next table. There, a group of women in their thirties were having an animated discussion and my friend overheard the words *great sex*. Now, he was only half-listening to his mother, and focusing his attention on the conversation at the next table.

"It turned out they're talking about their kids in grade six," he wrote.

I know exactly how he feels.

24

A Graduation That's About
Triumph and Courage

June 27, 2009

It was a high school graduation, but there was no prom dance. No tuxedos, though one or two guys had on ties. No fancy ball gowns on the women, but you could tell they had taken care to look nice that day. It was high school graduation, without the high school.

It was the graduation of the College and Career Preparation Program at Mohawk College and the simple room at the Fennell Campus was filled with students and their families. Not just happy moms and dads, though there were a few of those in the room, but husbands and wives and young children and even babies.

"I almost can't believe we made it to this day," said the woman sitting next to me, with a laugh. "But I'm glad we're here."

So were the graduates, and not in the usual, I'm-so-happy-high-school-is-finally-over way. Because these were people who had found their way back to school and that journey was not an easy one. There were grey-haired men and women in their fifties, caught off guard when their work world disappeared right under their feet, women holding babies or sitting with toddlers, their education interrupted by life and all its surprises. And a group of young boys and girls, on the verge of being men and women, too old to go back to regular high school and too young and uneducated to make a life that worked.

There were valedictorian speeches. A man named Chris told the audience how a workplace accident had landed him back in school and how grateful he was to the teachers who worked hard with him and his classmates, often one-on-one, pushing them through the dark days of math classes and long, gruelling grammar lessons. How he wouldn't have made it without their encouragement and understanding, their willingness to listen, even when the problems had nothing to do with algebra or English lit.

A tiny woman named Marjorie joined Chris at the front to tell her story, and when she came to the part where she too wanted to thank the teachers and the staff of the program, her voice broke and she turned her back to the audience and wept. "I'll read it for you," said Chris, and he did, and her words of gratitude filled the room.

Jim Vanderveken, the director of the program, told the graduates they should be proud of what they had accomplished. That he knew how hard it was for many of them to face a classroom after so many years; how intimidated and anxious they felt coming back to school.

He told them he knew how much courage and determination it took to get to this day. And when I glanced over at my wife beside me, I saw the tears rolling down her face. She was crying for every student in that room, and for our son James, who was one of them.

Life has a way of interrupting our best-laid plans. For James, a series of major surgeries and the long recoveries that followed threw him off course. He tried. God knows we tried. But it just didn't work, and when time had passed and his body and mind had healed enough, he found himself too old, perhaps too changed, to go back to a high school classroom.

And so he went to Mohawk College, on his own, to a classroom every day, where he worked hard at unravelling the mysteries of calculus and geometry. And every day, his teachers, "Mr. Rufus" and Tina, would work hard with him, joking and cajoling, and encouraging him through the months and months of study. Until this day, when we watched him walk up and get his diploma. And, as each and every student did that, the room burst into applause and whoops and whistles.

And if pride in accomplishment was rocket fuel, there was enough in the room that day to take each and every one of them to the moon.

25

Memories of Dad Can Bring Tears

August 8, 2009

My dad died one year ago today, August 8. My mom will likely get everyone together for a dinner. Maybe they'll order Chinese food, she said. But I won't be there. I'll be on holiday with my family. I don't know what we'll do that day; perhaps we'll raise a glass to him. Maybe I'll say something, but I don't know for sure.

Anyone who has lost a parent knows what happens afterward is a bit odd. For a while after Dad died, I wasn't sure how I felt. People would ask if I was all right and I'd say, "Yeah, I'm fine," but that wasn't entirely true. I wasn't sad exactly; I was just kind of flat. Life goes on and you have to go on with it, and you do, but there's something a bit off-kilter about it all.

Take Father's Day. My mom phoned me and said, "I'd like to do something for Father's Day," and I thought, *Like what exactly? Our dad's dead. Won't that be kind of weird?* But what I said was, "Sure, Mom, whatever you like." Well, what she liked was that we would all go to the cemetery that morning and "visit" my dad. I have to admit I thought this was almost funny, because pretty much the last place you would ever find my father on a Sunday morning was the cemetery. He didn't like them much and he didn't see the point in going there. He had a line he liked to use: "It's better to visit people when they're alive. They appreciate it more." He dutifully visited his aunts and uncles and cousins, often on Sundays, but after they died, I really don't remember him ever going to their graves.

So, it was a bit strange to get all the kids together and drive out along Plains Road to the cemetery to "visit" Dad on Father's Day. But my mother wanted us to, and who says no to their eighty-one-year-old mother anyway? Everyone showed up and we milled around and tended to the gravesite and read headstones and generally stood around talking. But we really didn't talk about our father, and even at dinner, nobody made a toast or said anything. There wasn't really much to say. It was Father's Day and our father wasn't there.

Actually, I find the "event" days — Christmas and Easter and Father's Day and the rest — not that tough. It's the other times, when you're in the car alone driving to work in the middle of the week and some small thing makes you think of your dad and your stomach does a flip, and before you know it tears are streaming down your face and you have to swallow hard and grip the wheel and you feel a bit like an idiot driving down the 401 crying. And then, as fast as it came, it passes, like those quirky summer showers, and you feel okay again, but just a little hollow inside.

And sometimes I wonder if it's just me and I don't really ask my pals who have lost their fathers in the last few years if they cry on the way to work because, well, because you just don't do that. But I was at a wedding recently and the brother of the groom got up and was giving a killer speech — all smart and clever and breezy — and he got to the line where he wanted to mention something his father once told him and he said the word *dad*, and in that second his voice caught and his face crumpled and he stood there in front of a roomful of people and unstoppable tears rolled down his face.

"I'm sorry," he said, wiping the tears away, but he didn't have to apologize because everyone in that room who has lost someone close knows that, at any time and often when you least expect it, we're all just a word or a memory or a moment away from tears.

26

Going, Going Lawn

August 22, 2009

Last week I walked over to my neighbour Dave's to borrow a cup of gasoline.

"Hi, Dave. I need a cup of gasoline," I said to him when he opened his front door.

"Are you sure you don't mean gin?" he said, knowing me well.

"No, I need some gas for your lawn mower. It's empty."

I had already gone over and "borrowed" Dave's lawn mower, which sits at the side of his house and is easy pickings for neighbours like me. I have to say, though, that I was quite disappointed to find it almost empty. What's wrong with people? Do they think I have time to fill up their lawn mowers?

I was back stealing Dave's lawn mower again not because I do not have a lawn mower. I do. Actually, I have three. But lately, I have been experiencing a common problem for men over fifty — MLD — Multiple Lawn Mower Dysfunction.

Let me explain.

First I had an electric lawn mower. Personally, I feel these were built as an engineering frat party joke. Think about it. You're trying to cut your lawn with something that's plugged in to a wall. It's pretty much like taking an electric fan to work on a twenty-kilometre extension cord. I have to admit, though, I found it quite easy to use:

1. Plug in lawn mower.
2. Start lawn mower.
3. Drive over cord.

So, I found myself back at Dave's, but this time he was ready for me. "Here is my parents' old Toro. You can have it, if you promise to stop coming over and bothering us," he said.

"Deal," I said, knowing I would be over there later for dinner with the old "we've run out of propane for our barbecue" line. This has worked several times, and Dave has not seemed to notice that we actually have a natural gas line for our barbecue.

Dave's parents' lawn mower was a perfectly good machine — in 1976. Now, all you have to do to get it going is to pull the starter cord three or four hundred times. Once it's running, you can cut as much as two feet of grass before the motor quits and you have to restart it. After a couple hundred pulls, and a fair amount of swearing, it starts smoothly and you can cut another full square foot of grass before it stalls again. On a hot summer day, this process seems to attract a lot of attention, and before you know it, there's a small crowd of neighbours standing around asking if everything is okay or if you would like something — perhaps a glass of water or an ambulance.

My neighbour across the street who is retired and has a lot of free time to make fun of me said, "Did you mix the right amount of oil in the gasoline?"

Oil? Who said anything about oil? If they need oil, why do they call them "gas" lawn mowers? I thought. Out loud, I replied, "I'm not sure."

"Well, the correct fuel mixture is usually fifty to one," he added, helpfully.

Fuel mixture? What is this, a NASA launch? I just want to cut my lawn. I put away the Toro.

The other lawn mower I have was left by the neighbours when they moved a few months ago. "It needs a bit of work," they said.

I may have left it outside in the rain for several months, but in the spring I told my wife that I thought it was a good lawn mower and that I would "tinker" with it.

"Are you insane?" she replied. "First, you don't have any tools, unless you count nail clippers. Second, you can barely load a stapler by yourself. Third,

I will kill you if I see another broken-down lawn mower within a hundred miles of this house."

Upon closer inspection, I noticed the lawn mower appeared to be fused by rust into a solid mass.

A few days later, I found a used but working lawn mower in my driveway. (No kidding.) I've checked around but no one has owned up to giving it to me. So, to the Lawn Mower Fairy of Flatt Avenue — Thanks! And one more thing: do you have any gas?

27

Fall Fair Affair

October 17, 2009

Every year about this time our whole family goes to a fall fair.

We make this annual pilgrimage for a variety of reasons, including ecological awareness, community building, and the chance to see a squash that's bigger than Michael Ignatieff's ego.

Generally, though, we go to the fair as a break from the non-stop eating we do on Thanksgiving weekend.

Because both my wife and I have large families (I mean large in number, not large in size — sorry, Mom), we end up eating two entire Thanksgiving meals in two days, resulting in the ingestion of our own body weight in turkey, gravy, and pumpkin pie. Hundreds of hours at the Y can be wiped out in one meal.

Okay, it's a four-hour meal and that doesn't include appetizers. This year, we had (no kidding) nine pies on the table. Many people used the line "Oh, I'll just have a sliver — of ALL of them."

It's difficult to estimate caloric load when you're dealing with foods made entirely of whipped cream and animal lard, but if Weight Watchers points were Air Miles our whole family could fly to Singapore and back for free.

So, fall fairs give us a chance to push ourselves away from the table, get in the car, and drive to the fair — and start eating again.

I love fall fairs, and I especially love the Norfolk fall fair in Simcoe, which we have attended faithfully for twenty years. I can get pretty excited about going to the fair. There's something about the unmistakable scent of cotton candy and horse manure that makes me lose my head.

(True Story Ahead Alert.)

One year, I was in such a rush to get to the fair that I parked the family van and jogged over to the fairgrounds. When we returned to the car several hours later, my young nephew looked at the van and said, "Hey Uncle Paul, how come smoke is coming out of your car?" It seems in my haste to get to the llama exhibit, I had left the car running all afternoon. Not only did I burn through $50 worth of gas, but our carbon footprint for the day was just slightly less than Alberta's.

Now, on my wife's insistence, we pause in the parking lot to ensure that the vehicle is off and that we have not left any children or pets in the car. She's such a stickler for detail.

Why do I love the fair? First, there are the animal barns. Where else can you see a grown man lovingly blow-drying a large cow (okay, not counting the Internet). There are pigs the size of cows, horses the size of dogs, and birds that can puff up bigger than Stephen Harper's hair.

Where else is fried dough and sugar a major food group? Call them all the cute names you want — funnel cakes, beaver tails, or elephant ears — they're just disguised giant doughnuts, and they're fooling no one.

Where can you eat all day and never encounter anything green — unless you get a really old corn dog? There's pork on a bun, bacon on a bun, pulled pork, perogies, pitas, pizza, and poutine — and that's the health food. Don't forget cotton candy, candy apples, fudge, beer nuts, salt water taffy, and sugar-coated pepperoni sticks. (All right, I made up the last one, but it's actually not a bad idea.)

The fair also boasts many educational elements for the kids. For example, the carnies can teach you about games of chance and why good dental hygiene is important.

The midway rides are an excellent opportunity to discuss risk assessment, or why you may want to think twice about getting on a very fast, two-storey-high ride that was assembled by guys who smell like they spent the night at a Captain Morgan party and then slept in a dumpster.

And then there are the displays of giant pumpkins. This year's winner weighed 1,450 pounds, and in the right light bore a striking resemblance to Mike Duffy.

I also love the commercial building. We left with a magic veggie peeler, the ShamWow!, a coupon for a vibrating chair, and bee ointment guaranteed to make you taller.

And the great thing is that no matter how full the parking lot is, I can always find my car.

It's the one that's smoking.

28

There's Always a Part of You That Feels Eighteen

October 31, 2009

When I called my mother last week, she was too busy to talk to me. "I'm rehearsing," she said. "I've joined a dance troupe."

This was pretty much like her saying she'd joined the Ringling Brothers Circus. Not that she hadn't been a good dancer, but I didn't expect to see her on *So You Think You Can Dance* anytime soon. Besides, she's eighty-two.

"Sorry, Mom, can you explain that? And go slowly."

When my mom gets excited she tends to speak quickly and to leave out the first sentence or two of the conversation. This saves a lot of time, but often I have virtually no idea what she's talking about. So it sounded like this: "Jill says our costumes have to be ready for the dress rehearsal and opening night is Thursday and tickets are going fast so how many do you want?"

"Who's Jill? What performance? What tickets? What costume?"

It was almost lunchtime and I was wondering if Mom had been dipping into the vino pail my brother got for her. You know, you gotta wonder why a hundred-pound grandmother needs a five-gallon plastic barrel of wine in her house, but that's another story.

It turns out she really did join something called The Jill Schofield Dancers and she was going to be part of the annual Fall Fling at the retirement village where she now lives. And she was pretty excited about it.

Of course, it's important to know that my mother may well be the most enthusiastic person in the world. She can get pumped up about almost anything — from darning socks she finds at our place to baking cookies for the village Wednesday coffee hour. A while ago the phone rang at 8:30 on Saturday morning. "I've finished those socks if you want to come and pick them up," she said excitedly. I explained that I was still in my underwear and could not rush right over. She understood, but sounded a bit disappointed.

Anyway, last week my brothers and sisters and I found ourselves in a crowded room in the old barn at St. Elizabeth Village, nervously awaiting the start of what turned out to be a three-hour variety show with the range of the Ed Sullivan Show, the good nature of Tiny Talent Time, and the jokes of a Las Vegas lounge act.

You could call it a nice "family show" if your family included Mae West, Hugh Hefner, and Buddy Hackett — as the Beaver. There were songs you hadn't heard in years — such as "If I Give My Heart to You," sung beautifully by a tiny woman named Fran, and things you've never seen in your life, like Lou, a woman who sat in an armchair and perfectly whistled "Edelweiss." There were old guys in full drag, including Frank, who had surprisingly nice legs for a ninety-five-year-old.

There were short skits — mostly about sex and getting old and, as a change of pace, about getting old and sex. There was everything from the rousing Good News Singers choir belting out Maritime church songs to a handsome guy named Ervin whose Elvis impersonation prompted several women to throw their underwear at him. I'd call them panties if panties were the size of Dundas.

There were also trembling hands and trembling voices, some missed dance steps and missed notes, song lyrics that momentarily escaped memory, and song notes that just slipped out of range. There were ladies standing close, arm in arm, reading from the same handwritten lyric sheets, and men carefully helping a friend safely make that one tricky step off the stage. And amid all the applause and laughter, it became clear that no matter how old you are, there's always a part of you inside that feels eighteen, even if it's just for one night.

And there was my mom, dressed in an orange poodle skirt she made herself and white bobby socks dancing away to "Wanna Bop with You Baby," smiling and having more fun than she has had in the entire year since my dad died last summer. And though I know that there's a part of her that will forever be sad, it was tightly packed away this night, forgotten in a swirl of music and makeup and laughter. And life.

29

A Celebration of Life

January 9, 2010

Recently I was at a funeral where a birthday party broke out.

With a cake. And lighted sparklers and everyone singing "Happy Birthday."

People snapped pictures and the woman whose birthday we were celebrating was smiling and laughing as she blew out the candles — even though the funeral was for her mother.

It was, for sure, odd and oddly beautiful. Let me explain.

My aunt "Toni" — her real name is Antoinette and even though the last thing most Italian families need is another person named Tony that's what we called her. That's what everyone called her.

Except her husband, who called her Sam, for reasons no one can remember now.

Last month, Aunt Toni, my mom's last living sister, became ill with pneumonia and was in hospital in Niagara Falls. She had moved from Hamilton to Niagara Falls after she married my Uncle John more than forty-five years ago.

After my uncle died in the late nineties and my aunt was no longer able to take care of their little home, we helped her clean out the house and moved her into a retirement home not far from her neighbourhood and her ever-helpful sister-in-law Helen. And not far from her daughter, Julia Mary, who lived in a group home a few blocks away.

Julia Mary is developmentally delayed. Born prematurely, she had cerebral palsy and was partially blinded by the oxygen in the incubator where she spent the first few months of her tenuous young life. She had hearing problems and, as a child, she suffered almost endless grand mal seizures, which sent my aunt and uncle to the hospital more times than anyone could, or would want to, remember.

The doctors told them that Julia Mary was unlikely to live to be a teenager, and God knows she almost died so many times we lost count.

But she did not die.

And my aunt and uncle took care of her every single day for as long as they possibly could. And that was no small task, for as each year went by, they grew a year older, but Julia Mary was frozen in time, forever a pleasant and loving and excitable three-year-old.

And as my aunt aged and Julia Mary grew older, their lives began to mirror each other's. Both moved into homes surrounded by people like them and by helpful staff, and they both seemed happy.

Over the years when we visited at the home, it became clear that Aunt Toni was getting weaker. She moved slowly, used a walker to get to the dining room, and was sometimes a bit confused, but she always happy to see us and to chat over a cup of tea.

So, when a few weeks ago we went to visit her in the hospital, we were struck by how small and frail she had become, her broomstick-thin arms covered in skin as fine as tissue paper. The IV needles had bruised them, leaving dark red patches like spilled ink.

And though my mother, ever optimistic, talked about a new nursing home and personal-care workers, and maybe even moving her to Hamilton, I think we all knew that Aunt Toni, whose steely determination had given her amazing energy in life to care for her daughter and husband, would probably not be going anywhere.

A few days after that last visit, on December 19, she died in her sleep. She was eighty years old.

She would, in that funny, random, or perhaps not so random, way that life has, be buried on her daughter's birthday. And that's how we found ourselves three days before Christmas, on a blustery, icy-cold day, standing by her graveside and saying goodbye to an aunt who was as close to a mother as any aunt could be.

At the reception, Julia Mary was, of course, sad and subdued, but happy to be surrounded by her relatives and friends, and even at forty-four years of age, she was excited about her birthday. She squealed with delight at the sparklers, and after she blew out the candles and the cake was taken away to be cut, she paused for a moment and then turned to those around her. "Mommy gone to heaven, right?"

Yes, Julia, Mommy gone to heaven.

30

Anybody Know Where My Meat Went?

April 3, 2010

You might think it would be difficult to lose meat. I mean, it's not exactly like misplacing your wallet or your keys. You don't say, "Hey honey, did you see my prime rib roast around? I know I left it here somewhere." And yet, it is possible to forget where you put meat. I know because last weekend I had The Day of the Missing Veal.

Now, please do NOT write to tell me that you are against veal. Or beef. Or all meat and meat products, all animal products, leather, fur, gelatin, shoe horns made of real horn (okay, even I'm against those) — in fact, that you are against EVERYTHING that is not made of tofu, including couches, car upholstery, and wallets. (I did find a lovely tofu wallet at a local free-trade-whole-food-gift-shop-and-organic-car-insurance-co-op, but I got hungry and ate it.)

I am Italian and I am all for veal. Veal cutlets, veal sandwiches, veal hats, whatever, I love veal. And, listen, cows WANT to be veal. On a recent trip to Italy I spoke to some cows and they told me, "*Noi vogliamo essere il vitello,*" or roughly translated, "This is really boring. We'd rather be sandwiches."

In any case, the reason I was making veal is that my younger son, Matthew, had just returned from a school trip to Spain and Portugal and requested a special dinner. I found this a bit odd seeing as how he had spent that last ten days eating in restaurants in Barcelona, Madrid, and Lisbon, while we had been at home pretty much existing on Kraft Dinner, trying to pay for his flight and hotels.

"Matt," I said, "when I was a kid our March Break trip was a drive to Stoney Creek. For an ice cream cone. And I mean an ice cream cone — for five kids. It wasn't pretty. The back seat of the car was a like a scene from Wild Kingdom. When I told my dad I wanted an overseas adventure, he told me to join the armed forces. We all had to sleep in one ..."

At this point I noticed Matt had fallen asleep, as he often does during reminiscences about my childhood.

In any case, I found myself at the grocery store buying a few kilos of veal, which, thank god, happened to be on sale. I know I bought it because I have a distinct memory of the Italian guy in front of me buying seven pounds of veal. He may have been celebrating the Festival of St. Vitello, the Patron Saint of the Veal Sandwich, but I'm not sure.

In any case, the next day I could NOT find the veal. I checked the fridge, I checked the freezer. This is not as easy as it sounds because our freezer is filled with dozens of bags of unidentifiable food matter that we carefully put into unmarked, undated freezer bags. We use these for a fun family game we call Guess WHAT's Coming to Dinner? Many of the bags are frosted-up misshapen blobs of brownish-red stuff that could be tomato sauce, curried lamb, or a pile of pink rubber erasers in motor oil. It's kinda hard to tell. What I could tell was that there was no veal there.

Then I wondered if I had stored the veal over in my neighbour Dave's freezer because ours was full of, well, unidentifiable stuff.

I also wondered if perhaps Dave, who occasionally comes over and "borrows" all my new magazines, might have simply mistaken the veal for a particularly thick issue of GQ and taken it home.

I went over to his house and pointedly asked if he had my veal.

For some reason, he found this odd and thought I should go home and lie down. I did, and when I woke up later, I opened the freezer only to find the veal sitting on the middle shelf tucked under a bag of frozen corn.

I cooked it with some reddish stuff from a freezer bag. I thought it was pretty good, but Matthew said, all things considered, he'd rather be in Spain.

31

The Letter

April 17, 2010

I had forgotten about the letter.

I had meant to get to it, but so many other things got in the way. There was my tax return that I promised my wife I would finish a week ago, still sitting in a pile on the side table. I find doing my taxes a lot like Canadian elections — no matter how you juggle the numbers, the returns are always disappointing. So, there it sat.

And then there were all the other household chores that I'm in charge of — drinking coffee, lounging around, napping, pulling wine corks, it's all pretty exhausting. So, now it was 8:00 a.m. on Saturday and I had to write the letter for my daughter, Ella.

It's called a confirmation letter. Confirmation, for non-Catholics out there, is the sacrament kids get when they are about twelve or thirteen years old. It signals their acceptance into the church as reasoning, mature young adults.

(The sacrament doesn't see them giggling hysterically in the van or screaming "OhMyGod, he's so HOT!" through pretty much all of *Twilight*.) It's sort of the Catholic version of a bar mitzvah (more drinking at the party, smaller cheques in the envelopes) or a Native Spirit Walk, without the danger, unless you consider the very real risk of one of the little cousins barfing on you after eating the unwise combination of several cannoli and a gallon of Orange Crush.

The letter, which they read during an all-day retreat, is supposed to be a message from parents about confirmation and life and, well, everything. Try figuring that out at eight in the morning in your pyjamas. And so I sit at the computer, my hands frozen, my head searching for what to say to my thirteen-year-old daughter. We have done this before, for our two sons, but this morning the words do not come. "Tell her we love her," my wife calls from the other room.

And so I do. I tell her that we can hardly believe that she is already here, grown up, ready for confirmation, graduation and, soon, for high school. That, in many ways, I still think of her as the toddler who used to hide behind her mother's legs when people came to the house. That I still see the little curly-haired girl who would literally shake at the sight of a dog, even the tiny Boston Terrier from the up the street. That I sometimes have to remind myself that the tall, beautiful girl I bump into in the hallway in the morning is her, and not the knee-high girl standing next to me in the photograph that sits on her bedside table. I tell her that she is beautiful inside and out. That her mother and I marvel at all the gifts she's been given — a good brain, a healthy body, and, most of all, a big heart.

As I'm writing, I realize these rituals are important, not so much in themselves, but because they give us a chance to tell our children all the things we mean to say to them, but that in the busy rush of the days and months and even years, we never quite get to. And in doing that, we're forced to remind ourselves what counts, and to think hard about what we really care about in life. And so I tell her that, starting with the most obvious and most important thing every kid needs to hear.

"We love you. Your brothers love you (even if they steal your iPod and complain about the number of showers you take!), and you are surrounded by a loving family of aunts, uncles, cousins, and grandparents and many friends. In a way, an army of love and support stands behind you as you march into the next part of your life.

"Life is a wonderful journey, Ella. We know you are setting out on that journey now, leaving childhood behind you, and though we will miss the little shy girl with the big smile, we stand here, amazed at the beautiful young woman you have become.

"Go forward with our love and support to propel you, and be ready to love and be loved and to embrace all the wonders this life has to offer."

32

Memories Spring Up in My Garden

June 12, 2010

I am trying to grow vegetables in the garden this summer.

That's a problem for several reasons. One, we don't have a garden. Our backyard is a carefully cultivated blanket of weeds augmented by poorly maintained shrubbery, and a picnic table usually festooned with a stunning assortment of empty beer bottles courtesy of my eldest son and his pals, who I think are secretly employed by Brewers Retail to drive beer sales in Ontario.

The second reason a garden is an unlikely proposition is the extent of my gardening experience, which is as follows: I have eaten a "garden" salad on occasion and visited the Garden Gallery several times. The few plants I have bought usually die — often on the way home — or are killed slowly over the course of the first few weeks of summer.

Last year I inadvertently "waterboarded" one lone tomato plant to death. (It told me nothing.)

But this year, I went out and bought three small beefsteak tomato plants and put them out into the backyard. While I was digging them in and carefully tying their stems to stakes, I couldn't help but think about my father.

For years he planted a full garden — tomatoes, garlic, onions, peppers, string beans, zucchini, arugula, lettuce, basil, rosemary, and parsley. He'd tend to the plants every day and, especially after he retired, he'd put in hours pruning, clearing the weeds, and carefully watering everything. It wasn't exactly The Godfather or anything, but he would spend long happy afternoons out there keeping that garden in shape.

Funny, too, because my dad did not, in most ways, fit the popular Italian stereotype. He couldn't build a thing, never laid a brick in his life, didn't know a cement mix from cake mix, and had no idea how to set tile. But he had fond memories of the farms and vineyards near his hometown in Italy, and he loved gardening and the idea of growing his own food. And he was good at it, producing enough vegetables to feed our whole family all summer long.

But one afternoon, he may have taken this notion of "living off the land" a bit too far.

That day, we came home to find him sitting in the kitchen holding a piece of string in his hand and staring intently out through the back door.

The string led out to the yard to a four-inch stick upon which our screen door was carefully balanced. Underneath was a scattering of chunks of day-old bread. This is probably a good time to mention that most Italians love game birds — uccelli — but not for their beautiful plumage or soothing calls. No, they love them slow cooked and served with polenta, and my father was no exception.

You didn't have to be an Inuit trapper to figure out what was going to happen next. When enough blackbirds for dinner had gathered under the door, my dad pulled the string and then walked out into the yard, hammer in hand. My sisters screamed, my brothers clapped (who knew Dad was a great hunter?), and my mother put on the boiling water.

After a few hours of cleaning, plucking, and sautéing, we sat down to a delicious dinner.

I think my dad thought this might be a weekly feast — vegetables AND meat from the back garden! — until our next-door neighbour Mrs. Cooper got wind of things.

The fact that her yard was filled with bird feeders might have given Dad a small clue about what her reaction would be to his new hunting practices.

A short over-the-fence conversation convinced him it might be more prudent just to buy some quails at the local butcher.

So, on this hot summer Saturday I plant the tomatoes with an equal mix of nostalgia and hope, and with the unsettling recognition that despite our sometimes misguided intentions and misplaced efforts to be different, we end up more like our parents than we ever imagined.

I smile thinking about my dad holding that string, but I know that, unless interest rates really go up, the birds around here are safe.

33

A Thule and His Sanity Are Soon Parted

July 10, 2010

I had a feeling it was going to be an odd weekend, just based on the note my wife sent around.

She was trying to organize the meal plan for Canada Day and the weekend. When you have three families going up to the cottage with assorted kids, friends, and other visitors, you have to plan or you'll end up with a steady diet of hot dogs, chips, and pop. And by pop, I mean beer.

So, the email went out, lining up breakfast, lunch, and dinner duties, with a quick reminder at the bottom: "Everyone bring snakes and booze. How does that sound?" It sounds like a bad combination, second only to "guns and booze" on my list of bad ideas. Luckily, everyone brought Cheetos instead of reptiles, and the weekend, at least food-wise, proceeded without incident.

I wish I could say the same for every other aspect. First, because we were bringing three of my daughter's friends with us and we don't own a school bus, we had to figure out space for luggage. That meant getting out the dreaded Thule and attaching it to the top of the car. A Thule, for those of you intelligent enough to keep your luggage IN the car, is a large plastic container shaped like a flattened egg that hooks on to your vehicle and tricks people into thinking you ski.

Though a reasonable person might think Thule is pronounced Thool (as in "fool") they'd be wrong. It's actually pronounced "Two-Lee," because the Swedish think it's clever to have a language that defies all human understanding and sounds funny.

So, we attached the Thule to the roof of the car, a surprisingly simple operation considering these are the same people who put out Ikea furniture, which no living person outside of Sweden can actually assemble. I have one word for the Swedes — "screwdriver." Normal people do not build furniture with something called an Allen key. It's unnatural.

Anyway, we loaded the Thule with all our clothes and most of the food and then locked it and double checked that it was securely fastened to the roof. This is important. In the first day of ownership of the Thule, my wife tested its structural integrity by driving fairly rapidly into the underground parking lot at McMaster Medical Centre while wondering, "What is that loud noise?" After several attempts to enter the lot, she noted that the alarmed expression on the kiosk guy's face AND the loud noise were directly related to her forward motion. The Thule survived, though it had a nice big crack in it, and my wife now ducks instinctively anytime we drive into an underground parking lot.

So, we drove down to Lake Erie on a beautiful, sunny day, pulled up to the cottage, got out and realized that the key for the Thule was sitting on the dining room table back in Hamilton. This was okay if we wanted to wear the same shorts and T-shirt for four days and live on snakes and booze.

Naturally, we proceeded to do what any two mature adults would do. We: 1. Argued about who left the keys at the house; 2. Questioned whose "bright idea" it was to buy a bloody Thule in the first place; and 3. Said, "Why do we have a cottage? Why? And I hate your family."

After that, we attempted to open the Thule without the key. This time we used a more reasoned, scientific approach. I jiggled it vigorously while swearing, tried to force a screwdriver into the lock using more swearing and then attempted to simply break through the Thule's shell. What I learned from this process is that loud swearing has little technical effect (though it really attracts the neighbours) and that in the case of a nuclear attack, you will probably find me IN a Thule, later to join all the surviving Swedes for post-atomic fondue and hot-tubbing.

Finally, I suggested a more sane solution — using July 1 fireworks to blow the Thule to pieces — but my wife decided it might be more prudent to drive to Hamilton, get the key, and drive back out the cottage. I thought this was an excellent idea, wished her well, and went to lie down. I realized later we should have tried an Allen key.

The Man Who Cleared Out the West

August 7, 2010

Recently, I had a colonoscopy.

For those of you who have not had the experience, a little background may be necessary. A colonoscopy is a procedure in which a group of highly trained medical professionals take pictures in your bum. Not "of your bum" — for that, check Google Groups, probably somewhere between bowling and bungee jumping.

Anyway, like a lot of guys over fifty, I thought it was time somebody took a tour of my colon. So I booked the appointment months ago and before I knew it the day of reckoning was upon me.

I vaguely remembered there was some preparation involved, which I assumed to be fairly self-evident, something like "Avoid the Wednesday Fiery HOT Enchilada Special at Chi-Chi's," and the perennial direction to "wear comfortable clothing." I have never understood that last bit, since the first thing they ask you to do at the hospital is "remove all clothing" and put on a specially designed hospital gown that would be comfortable if you were heading out to the Annual Burford Buttocks Parade.

In any case, I found the instruction sheet that had the headline "Patient Instructions for Bowel Preparation." I had never prepared my bowel for anything, so I read the instructions carefully. Some were easy: "Stop eating flax seed three days prior to the examination." Luckily, I had given up flax seed for Lent several years ago (along with tofu and several TV series I never watched) and have lived a remarkably full life without it.

All that seemed easy until I came to the line that said to take two tablets of Dulcolax and a package of something called Pico-Salax. The latter comes with a warning that after you mix it with regular tap water, "If it heats up, let it cool down before drinking." I don't know about you, but I seldom drink anything that involves a chemical reaction producing HEAT. Call me crazy, but usually drinking something that is bubbling without any visible heat source is probably not a good idea.

Once you take all this stuff, you're encouraged to drink a LOT of water, and then there's this subtle warning: "Most people will have three to six bowel movements without urgently rushing to the bathroom." The person who wrote this NEVER took Pico-Salax.

It would be difficult to exaggerate the effect of this medication on your digestive system, but they could more accurately call it Colon Explosion. It's hard to describe what happens to you, but imagine eating a basket of cherries and drinking forty-two cups of coffee and then multiply by infinity. The phrase "without urgently rushing to the washroom" has about the same accuracy as "This will only hurt a bit" and "I will not raise taxes."

I'm not sure how most people define "urgently," but I would suggest it would be a HUGE MISTAKE to take this stuff and attempt to leave the house. In fact, my experience suggests that it's dangerous to even leave the bathroom. After living in your bathroom all day, you'll be pleased to know that the next instruction is to take the SECOND packet of Pico-Salax! All I can say is that by the time you are ready to go to the hospital, your colon is so empty they could build condos in it.

After this experience, the actual colonoscopy is pretty easy. That's largely because they give you drugs that relax you, and by "relax" I mean they could put a marching band in your bum and you wouldn't notice (except for maybe the tuba section).

In my case, I was lucky enough to be having a colonoscopy and an endoscopy at the same time, which meant the doctor was going to basically put a garden hose down my throat AND up my hooey in one afternoon. A nurse — and I am not making this up — asked, "Which one would you like to do first?" to which I replied, "That depends on whether they use the same hose."

Anyway, my very skilled and pleasant gastroenterologist, Dr. Barry Lumb, who in my nervousness I may have called Dr. Larry Bum, did an excellent job. I slept through most of it, though I do hazily remember watching a TV monitor which seemed to be playing a fusion of *Fantastic Voyage* and *The Secret Life of Sea Slugs*.

I'm happy to report that all is well and that I now have the title for a terrific western: *Pico Salax — The Man Who Cleared Out the West.*

35

Ah, Cottage Life …
A Second Home to Care For

August 21, 2010

In Canada during the summer — which can often last more than several entire days — everyone loves to go to the cottage.

By "everyone," of course, I mean everyone who does not own a cottage.

If you are visiting or renting a cottage, lucky you — this is pretty much all you need to do:

1. Buy hot dogs and hot dog buns. No one wants to eat a hot dog rolled in white bread or in a hamburger bun. No one can explain why.
2. Buy beer. (Always buy what you told your spouse you are going to drink and then double it.) Simply say, "I'm worried people might drop in" — as if anyone in their right mind would drive three hundred kilometres up north on a whim to "grab a beer with you."
3. Pack a bathing suit, T-shirt, shorts, and sandals. Don't bring anything else. No one cares what you wear on holiday, unless you are going to Muskoka, in which case, again, don't bring anything you have. It's not good enough. Just buy all new clothes when you get there. (Also, dye your kids' hair blond and call them Scooter or Biff no matter what their names are. It will help you fit in.)

Once you get up to your rented cottage, all you have to do is sit around, read, drink, and nap. If you are visiting a cottage, remember to bring an inexpensive "cottage-warming" gift. Even if it is really dumb and something you would not put in your garage, never mind your house — like a giant carved carp clock — it will guilt your hosts into not asking you to do anything while you are there.

On the other hand, if you own a cottage, then what you are doing is getting away from all the annoyances at your house, like lawn cutting, housecleaning, and your kids, and driving for several hours in traffic so that you can arrive at your cottage and enjoy a whole new set of annoyances.

First, it will take you several hours to unpack. This is because even if you are going up for a weekend, everyone brings enough supplies to survive a nuclear winter and to avoid something even worse than the complete destruction of the earth's biosphere: driving into town. That's right, you NEVER want to have "to drive into town" to pick up something you forgot.

> Husband: Honey, are you sure we really have to bring this one-hundred-pound bag of sugar?
> Wife: Yes, yes. If we run out, we'll have to drive into town!

There's actually a reason for this deep-seated fear of town. Most towns in cottage country have a population of 1,270, which increases slightly in the summer to four million. This means that if you can even get into town, you will be surrounded by thousands and thousands of people who forgot some vital cottage necessity — like bug spray or Bailey's Irish Cream. In Muskoka, not only will there be thousands and thousands of people, but all of them will be wearing almost identical pastel-coloured golf shirts and plaid shorts. This can be very disorienting.

In the end, one trip into town can take up most of the weekend, and sometimes guests who have to "go into town" simply don't come back and are never seen again.

If you don't have to drive into town, then you can "relax" with a bit of window cleaning, septic inspection, spider spraying, sink unplugging, lawn cutting, and wood chopping. Once that's done, inevitably your wife will want you to get to work on a few "small projects" she had in mind, like building a new guest bunkie or moving the shoreline "slightly to the right."

When you are done the cottage work, you might think it is time to relax and enjoy yourself, but you would be wrong. It's actually time to go home. This is because everyone wants to "get an early start" so that they can "beat the traffic." The result is that by 9:00 a.m. on Sunday the highway looks like the Saturday parking lot at Fortinos.

Luckily, it only takes four or five hours to get home, where you spend another hour or two unpacking the car.

But don't worry; soon you'll be able to relax — once you get to work on Monday.

36

Hunting the Wild Tinsel and Other Traditions

December 11, 2010

This year, once again, we have taken a pledge to not "overdo it" for Christmas.

This solemn promise, which often lasts several entire days, is only one part of our many Pre-Christmas Traditions. These are fun, family activities handed down for generations, or things we just made up last year.

They include:

1. Getting Out the Christmas CDs. These are actual CDs we bought with real money containing songs no one can stand for more than a few days without going insane. Johnny Mathis's "It's the Most Wonderful Time of the Year" has to be encased in a locked metal box, just to make sure it isn't inadvertently played by an unsuspecting child. (The CIA uses this song to extract confessions from terrorists who, after only three or four playings, will admit to liking Lady Gaga.)
2. Trying to Find the Box of Christmas Decorations — and Failing. This is a wonderful yearly activity the whole family can enjoy that promotes good cheer and attempted murder charges. Each January, my wife dutifully stores all the seasonal decorations in a large plastic tub, carefully labels it, and then makes the single biggest mistake a human can make. She gives it to one of our sons to "put in the basement." This is like throwing it into a landfill

site, only worse. (Landfill sites have bulldozers.) Typically, I have to go down to the basement and make my way into the area we laughingly refer to as the Storage Room, which is code for "Wow, I can't even get this friggin' door open!" I now tie a rope around my waist before entering because of an unfortunate incident a year ago that resulted in me missing work for several days until one of the kids found me while looking for an old Super Mario game. After several hours of rooting around and often finding something unexpected — "Hey, that's where we left Uncle Tony last year!" — I give up.

Then, we go out and repeat another annual tradition I lovingly call Re-buying All the Stupid Christmas Decorations. You know, you walk around stores purchasing things that under normal conditions would be generously described as "hideous." Dried twigs bent into the shape of a moose, plastic wreaths covered in sparkly fruit, nativity scene snow globes, and other tasteful items headed directly to the next garage sale.

Then we sit down for our Almost Final Pre-Christmas Tradition. I say "almost" because the last thing we always do is frantically wrap gifts on Christmas Eve until three in the morning. My wrapping ability is marginal at the best of times, and after few hours and several rye and gingers, I notice that the large, awkwardly wrapped gift in the corner is making gurgling noises, and I realize I have wrapped up my wife.

Anyway, each year we sit down and agree that we will show restraint at Christmas. This usually comes after what I would call a "less-than-festive" look at our bank statement warning us that our current household situation is a lot like Italy and Ireland's combined: good food, good stories, no money. Any more Christmas spending and we are going to be in a deep ho-ho-hole!

So, I suggested that instead of buying dozens of gifts, we would just buy One Big Item for each child. The kids agreed this was a great idea. Matthew asked for the state of Montana, but would settle for a big-screen TV. Ella thought an all-inclusive trip to Cuba would be nice, but only if she could bring a few friends. It was then that we realized our idea of something "big" was slightly different than theirs. Big for me meant something the size of a large recycling box or one of those oversized Toblerone bars. Clearly, we needed another strategy. So, my wife cleverly suggested we buy several hundred "smaller" gifts for each child, which to my mind sounded vaguely like what we always do.

"That sounds vaguely like what we always do, honey, and that means we'll end up spending the equivalent of an MP's expense account on each child again this year."

I lost the argument, but I know I'm getting something big for Christmas this year — the Visa bill.

37

A Gift of Long-Remembered Music

December 26, 2010

For weeks now, as I write this, our daughter has been busy preparing her Christmas present.

This is surprising behaviour and utterly unlike that of her two brothers who, much like their father, will dash around madly in the final shopping hours before Christmas vainly trying to find presents on a small budget and an even smaller gift-giving imagination. The results are predictable — a box of scented soap, an Old Spice gift set, a tie, maybe a set of steak knives. It's all okay, of course. It's the thought that counts, even if the thought comes late and without much funding to support it.

No, Ella is getting ready, but not in the usual way. She has not been saving her babysitting money or checking online catalogues. She has been practising — learning, slowly and sometimes arduously, the complicated and beautiful passages of Debussy's "Clair de Lune."

She does this almost every night, sitting at the piano in our living room; the same piano, a lovely Heintzman baby grand, that her grandmother played on many evenings many years ago. Ella never heard her grandmother play, but has heard countless times about the song she loved most, "Clair de Lune." One afternoon, a few months ago, Ella asked her mother to drive to the music store, where she bought the sheet music, then came home and began to practise.

Ella did not know her grandmother. My wife's mother, Elin, died suddenly at the age of forty-six. She suffered a brain aneurysm and was rushed to hospital, monitored for several days, and then operated on. After the surgery she never regained consciousness, and a few days later she died. When she passed on that July day in 1977, she left seven children, a husband, and an army of relatives and friends who loved her. My wife was only sixteen when her mother left this world, just a couple of years older than Ella is today.

Though Elin has been gone now for a long time, a vivid picture of her remains indelible in her children and in the people who knew her. Oddly, considering that she died more than three decades ago, she is spoken of often, and in a way that makes you sad if you did not know her. I have never once heard her name mentioned, by either men or women, without the word *beautiful* in the same sentence.

There are old photographs of her, though not many, and they show a slim blonde with fine features and large, blue eyes. In the pictures, she is often smiling. She was, by all accounts, a striking woman. When she was young, she did some modelling, and later, even while managing seven children and a busy household, she could, with a touch of lipstick and a hastily pulled-on dress, present a simple elegance that other women admired. But she was not only beautiful, she was fun. When people talk about her, they often mention her infectious laugh, her favourite cocktail, Scotch on the rocks, the signature string of white pearls around her neck, her sense of joy — she would sometimes perform an impromptu dance on the living room coffee table — her natural grace, and always, the elegant sound of her playing the piano.

She would, when the mood hit her, usually after dinner while the children cleared the table and washed the dishes, sit at the piano her father had given her, and play. And frequently, she would fill the house with the haunting, stirring strains of her favourite song, even a few bars of which today can instantly evoke her memory. Perhaps this is how people endure, in a passing hint of perfume, a familiar laugh heard across a room, in the smoky scent of Scotch whisky on a winter night, or in the rising notes of a haunting melody.

And so, this Christmas, when the dinner was done and the table cleared and the gifts opened, Ella gave her mother a present with no wrapping paper and no bow. She sat down at the piano and her fingers moved across the ivory keys, filling the room with music, with the soaring, shimmering sounds of "Clair de Lune." And a young woman brought back, if only for a fleeting moment, the grandmother she never knew for the mother she loves.

38

The Worst Angler Ever

July 23, 2011

Recently, while visiting our friends at Honey Harbour, I was up early and out on the dock fishing. I am not up early because I am a fishing hero, but mostly because I have to pee a lot, and once you're up, you may as well do something. So for the next two hours I cast, jig worms, try various lures, walk the shoreline, and basically use all my limited fishing knowledge and equipment to its fullest.

The only bites I get are from mosquitoes.

Eventually, my Hamilton neighbour Dave, who is also up for the weekend, wanders out to the dock, coffee in hand. "Any luck?" he asks. I explain that it is very likely that acid rain and overfishing have removed all known aquatic life from this area's ecosystem.

He nods. "Can I have a try? I like to just dangle my line right off the dock."

"Oh yeah, that's a good idea," I say, chuckling derisively as Dave winds his worm over and over again on the hook until it looks like an old shoelace. I point out that fish might not recognize it as a worm. "That's my style," he says.

Now I admit Dave knows a lot about many things such as weed control and martini mixing, but I realize then that he knows nothing about the art and science of angling. On top of that, he is dressed completely inappropriately for fishing. He's wearing crazy plaid L.L. Bean shorts, a white belt, and a white polo shirt. This would be normal cottage wear if we were at a place where people yell out, "I say Regis, fetch me more gin. And for God's sake man, ask Buffy if the tomato aspic is ready!"

So I leave Dave on the dock while I head up to get a coffee, muttering something about him being lucky if he catches a cold. While I am up there, I hear Annette, his wife, say in a singsong voice, "Oh Paul, you better get down here."

I come out of the cottage and cannot help but notice that Dave appears to be using my rod to try and lift an anvil out of the water. I suspect that he is caught on the boat prop, something I have done earlier and neglected to warn him about out of spite. "I have a fish on," he says calmly, with what I think might be a bit of a growing Cape Cod accent. I stumble down the rocks, spilling coffee all over myself, yelling out instructions. "Okay, Dave, back off him a bit. Don't reel so hard!" Excited, I drop to my knees to get a better look.

I squint into the water and notice what appears to be a small green boat under the dock.

"Cripes, that's one big fish! Take it easy, let him play out!" I bark out to Dave.

He glances down at me sprawled on the dock. "Relax, I've caught fish before."

After a few minutes, the bass lies out on the surface and I reach down and grab him. It's some fish, at least three pounds and probably better. Okay, it's pretty much bigger than any bass I've ever caught. We take some pictures of Dave with his fish and I ask him what he wants to do with it. "Oh, let's release him. We'll catch him next year."

Dave goes up and I spend the rest of the afternoon fishing in exactly the same spot as him. I even curl my worm up to look like a small worm pretzel like him. I have no shame. I just want to catch something. Of course, I catch nothing. The lake has returned to the fishless, barren wasteland it was when I started in the morning. I go in and put on plaid shorts so I can be more like Dave. Nothing works. Around dusk, my wife comes down and calls me in. "We're almost ready for dinner. People are starting to talk," she says.

At dinner, I graciously crown Dave the Weekend Fishing King, but I have a plan for next year.

First, I'm buying a white belt.

39

When I Put On His Ring, I Think of Him

August 20, 2011

Recently I did something I never dreamt I would do. I called my mother to bother her about jewellery.

I know this sounds odd, perhaps even unmanly, but I should admit that I often call my mother for advice. Say, for example, I spill a giant glass of red wine on our sofa after my wife has gone to bed. (Note to wife: this of course NEVER happened ever and is purely invented for demonstration purposes.) My mother will have several ways of removing this stain, and if those don't work, she will offer to sew a decorative pillow overnight to hide it by the morning.

She is extremely helpful, and despite her busy schedule of Senior Zumba classes, Coffee Hours, and Casino Days, she will often offer to do jobs that no sane person would dream of trying — such as taking a laundry basket full of random socks and trying to "match them."

This, of course, is not humanly possible, but it keeps her busy.

Anyway, back to the jewellery. I was calling to remind her that I wasn't getting any younger and that I was hoping to have some memento of my father.

My dad was not a jewellery guy at all, but he had a couple of rings, a watch, a name bracelet, and a few other small gold pieces he wore periodically.

I understood it was difficult for my mom to do this, but I reminded her that Dad had died more than two years ago and his stuff was still sitting in a drawer by her bed.

"It would be nice if each of the kids had something of his," I said.

So, a couple days later, when she came down for dinner, she handed me a small black suede pouch.

"Here, this is for you," she said quietly. Inside was a ring that my father would occasionally wear, usually when he was going out for an event, and one that I had always admired.

It was an odd piece, gold, with nine very rough-cut diamonds that looked like small chunks of quartz. The stones were cloudy and the gold dull, but I thought it was beautiful.

A few days later, I took the ring to a jeweller to be cleaned and repaired. Her eyes widened when I put the ring on the counter. "I've never seen a ring quite like this," she said, examining the filigree etching on the gold and the oddly cut diamonds. "It's really one of a kind."

I could not remember a time when my father did not have the ring, so I assumed he had brought it from Italy when he came after the war. My mother agreed, but even she did not know its origins.

So, we called my Zia Anita in Italy — my father's twin sister — and though she remembered the ring well, she could not quite recall if my father had inherited it from his father or if it had been a gift he received as a young man. "*Mi dispiace*," she said. "I'm sorry, but I can't remember, and anyone who would is dead."

I went to pick up the ring and when the young woman dropped it into my hand, I was speechless. The diamonds were not cloudy, they had simply been dirty. Now they sparkled in the light and the buffed gold gleamed.

"It's a beautiful piece," she said.

Last week marked the third anniversary of my dad's death. I did not go to the graveside and I did not feel bad about that. My father was never one for cemeteries, and though he understood why people paid their respects there, he rarely did.

But, there is probably not a day that goes by that I do not, in some small moment, think of my father — when I water the tomato plants in the morning, when I catch a glimpse of my hair greying the way his did, when I tell my daughter to "be careful" as she goes out the door each day.

And so, when I put on his ring, as I did this week, I think of him. And when people notice it and say, "My, that's quite a ring," I smile and say, "Yes, it used to be my father's."

111

40

Paul Puts the Pro in Procrastination

September 3, 2011

Everyone knows the saying, "A stitch in time saves nine," but few people know what it means. Including me, so I guess that's another of life's mysteries left unsolved.

Just kidding. What it really means is that you should repair something as soon as you notice it is damaged. Hence, a ripped shirt that needs a stitch is better fixed before it needs nine, which would be terrific if anyone alive still knew how to sew anything.

Mostly, if something breaks or needs repair, people just throw it out and get a new one. This is one reason I am very careful not to injure myself. I fear falling asleep one night and waking up in a cardboard box at the city dump. (Note to wife: I'm fine, really. Feel great.)

Unfortunately, we have not applied this wise saying to our own house. My operating philosophy about home maintenance is a carefully considered approach that involves what I like to call "Completely ignoring the problem until something falls and hits you." Even then I like to say, What's wrong with a few collapsing objects in the house? It can provide interest and excitement to an otherwise quiet day.

Despite my ideas, my wife decided it was time that a few things were fixed. For one, our bathroom fan had been partially detached and hanging from the ceiling for a little while. And by "a little while" I mean approximately twenty-seven months, give or take a year. It also had a bit of trouble working, and so every morning, when you switched on the bathroom lights, the fan took a while to get going, which sounded a lot like a used car trying to start in February. Only louder. When it finally did "turn over," it made as much noise as a medium-sized combine harvester, which meant our morning conversations were something like this:

"Goodmorning."

"What? I can't hear you!"

"I said GOODMORNING!"

"Sorry, what? Just a sec, I think it's warming up …"

Once we got out of the bathroom and regained our hearing, we had to go to our closets, where the lights inside had been out for some time. (For a definition of "some time," see above.) This meant trying to choose clothes in a completely dark, small room while rushing to get out of the house on time. Again, I thought this made dressing in the morning more of an "adventure," but my wife disagreed, particularly after an unfortunate incident where she went to work with a skirt on backwards and two different pumps.

So, she wrote up a list of "Needed Repairs!" that I promptly took action with, by putting it on the fridge with a magnet.

I thought this was a good step forward, but I lost momentum and the list remained there for "some time." (Again, see above.)

Then, this spring, a couple of stones on our front steps cracked and fell off. Again, I felt this added to the "charm" of the old stairs, noting that many historical objects, like the Coliseum or Joan Rivers, were basically "falling apart" and people still loved them. My wife disagreed, pointing out that both things had undergone massive structural repair — especially Joan Rivers.

I promptly took action by writing the word *stairs* on the list on the fridge. With this stride forward, I coasted for several more weeks and thought I was in the clear for August until several actual chunks of the stairway broke off, creating a small pile of rubble at the entrance to our house. This caused me to once again take charge — by calling my brother-in-law Woody.

He had a stone mason there the next day, and when I arrived home I found yellow caution tape across a large pile of sand and stones. (I wish

I were making this up.) I suggested that we could use the back door for a while, say until next spring, and then consider our options. Instead, Woody had a carpenter over who seemed to build an entire new staircase while I made coffee. The carpenter left me with one job — to prime and paint the stairs before winter.

No problem, I said. It's on the list.

41

An Empty Chair at the Dinner Table

October 15, 2011

I miss my son.

There, I've said it.

I've been pretending I'm not missing him. He left almost six months ago to work and travel in Europe. He'd graduated from high school and he wasn't sure what he wanted to do next, so he thought he would work abroad.

The kids call it a "gap year" — for most it's the space between high school and post-secondary.

Matt started talking about a trip during his "victory lap" at high school and he began saving money to make it happen. We weren't sure that he would actually pull it off, but he did. And in May he and a couple of pals boarded a plane for London with small wallets and big dreams.

My wife began missing Matt right away — actually starting on the drive back from the airport.

"That's impossible," I said. "He's only been gone forty-five minutes."

"You're insensitive," she said.

In the days and weeks and now months that he has been away, we've all missed Matt in different ways. Ella, his younger sister, is so busy with her fifteen-year-old, high school, volleyball, and friend-filled life that on most days I think she forgets that he's gone.

Except for the evenings when at the dinner table my wife would just say his name and Ella would suddenly burst out crying. "I miss Meeshie," she burbled through her tears, using a nickname from his childhood.

James, his older brother, misses him the way he does everything else — inside and quietly.

My wife, on the other hand, makes no effort to disguise her daily thoughts of our middle son. She's pretty much "lurking" him on Facebook, logging on each night after dinner to see "what's new."

Then, about every three or four days, when she can't stand it any longer, she Skypes Matt and puts him through the kind of grilling usually reserved for robbery suspects and breakfast sausages.

"Are you eating? You look a bit skinny," "You need to shave!" and "Who are those people in the new photos you posted?" This is code for: "Who is the young lady in the photos you posted?"

Matthew, usually talking in the hallway of the hostel he's living at in Edinburgh, tells her he's fine and carefully avoids anything else, which is probably just the way it should be.

He's been working — casual jobs catering, waitering, and dishwashing — and paying his own way.

But recently we sent him an "early Christmas gift" (this might be the second or third, so I think we're covered up to at least Christmas 2016) — a flight to Italy. We did this so that he could meet up with my sister Rosanne and her husband, Joe, who are chaperoning my eighty-four-year-old mother around Italy for a couple of weeks. They are visiting my father's twin sister, the last surviving sibling, and now the living memory of their shared past and the rich, colourful history of their family.

I have sat at her kitchen table and heard those stories and I knew that Matt would be enthralled to walk the streets of the town of Conegliano, where his grandfather grew up, and sit with his grandmother and great aunt and learn about who he is and where he comes from.

In his email you can almost hear his trademark enthusiasm: "We had dinner at Zia's. Was awesome. I've heard lots about our heritage and our family's past. So awesome … it's just so great being here, I couldn't ask for any more — this place, the family, the food — the girls! Good God. Thank you so much, Mum and Dad. It's fantastic. I hope one day we can all end up here. It would be lots of fun. Well, I'm in bed now. So talk to u soon, love u all."

Last weekend, for the first time in his life, and ours, Matthew was not with us for Thanksgiving dinner. It was a big night, with his aunts and uncles and cousins crowded around the table, and he was missed. I miss him every day and I would be happy if he were back at our table.

But I'm even happier he's not.

42

There's a Useless Antique in My House

March 3, 2012

Nobody calls me on the telephone anymore.

Well, that's not completely true. Nobody calls me on our "home phone."

I should probably explain to anyone under thirty that a home phone is an actual device about the size of a toaster that remains in your house. The reason you cannot take it with you to the bar, to your class, and into the toilet, where I'm sure you're receiving very important calls, is that it's attached by wires directly to the wall in your house. I know this sounds crazy, but these phones were invented by a Canadian named Alexander Graham Bell, who had an entire well-known company named after him — Graham Crackers Inc.

These old phones worked by transmitting your voice along copper wire using a scientific process called "I have no idea." Your phone is a cellphone or smartphone or "PDA," which is a group of parents that meet after school. These phones work without wires by a process known as "magic."

Because most young people are texting or BBMing, almost nobody is phoning anyone on their home phone because no one has one. Which is probably good because the way the economy is going, it's unlikely anyone under thirty will ever have a home to put it in. Anyway, the result is that our phone hardly ever rings and when it does, it sounds like this:

BRRRRRR! BRRRRR! (That's typing for a very loud ship's horn.) "Hel-lo. You have just won a free cruise to an unnamed and dangerous

Central American country. Call now to get more details on your free trip. You only have five minutes to respond. Press one to …"

I don't know what happens after this because I always hang up. Now, I hang up after the first "BRRRRRR!" It's hard for me to believe that anyone on the planet would sign up for a cruise from a robot voice, but then again, there are people who think Rick Santorum should be president of a real country, so anything's possible.

The second call is an almost endless variation of this:

"Hello, may I speak with Mr. Ben, Mr. Bene … Benespaghetti?"

"Hello, is Mr. Bendoodie there?"

"Hello, Mr. Bed Netti?"

I always answer these honestly and directly: "I'm sorry, there is no one here with that name."

Some callers are more clever, using a question that gets around the name tongue twister:

"Hello. Am I speaking with the man of the house?"

To this, I usually respond: "Is this a trick question?" or "I'm not sure. You'll have to talk to my wife about that."

Another way around the name problem is to simply go with:

"Hello. May I speak to the homeowner?"

"Sure," I say, and give them the number of my bank.

I also have a very active social phone life that includes:

People calling me to give them old clothes.

People calling me to remind me to put out the old clothes.

People calling me disappointed that their driver came by and could not find the old clothes.

People calling me to give them old clothes again.

Based on the number of calls like this I get per week, it seems that people in these organizations think most Canadians have a small warehouse stacked with old clothes and second-hand appliances.

I have also received about seven hundred calls from a company we'll call "SeedMan," about my lawn. I never pick up, but I feel like we're friends now.

Because of these kind of extremely interesting calls on the home phone, no kid in the house ever bothers to answer it. Of course, all of them have expensive cellphones with monthly plans that could pay for an apartment. They need these phones to "keep them safe," my wife explained to me. Yes, I said, it keeps them safe from answering the home phone.

Anyway, we have talked about not having a home phone, but to me, it seems like a traditional part of Canadian family life — like a dining room table or a dangerously high line of credit.

So, don't worry, we're keeping our home phone and, yes, Mr. BeneDoodle will put the old clothes out on the porch.

If not, just call me.

43

I'm a Father. I Worry.

March 17, 2012

Not too long ago, in a moment of medium-depth insight of which I am occasionally capable, I came to the realization that I am almost always worried.

Not so much worried about the impending global environmental catastrophe or my less-than-adequate retirement savings or the always imminent viral pandemic, although those are worrisome enough.

No, I realized I'm always worrying about the kids.

I'm worried about the one who is abroad and the one who's at home. I'm worried about the one who's in high school, the one who's in college, and the one who isn't in any school at all. I worry about the one who goes out a lot and the one who doesn't. I worry about the one who has a driver's licence (I hope he's careful), the one who still doesn't have a driver's licence (What decade, exactly, is he going to get one?), and the youngest, who will be eligible for one next year (How can you drive when you always have one hand on your iPhone? Maybe by then, there'll be a Drive app).

I worry about them getting into college or university and I worry about what they are going to do there. My friends, many of whom have kids who have already graduated from university, worry about what they are going to do next.

In some ways, I'm a bit surprised I'm this worried. I admit I am not a particularly doting father. I have never believed that once you have a child, your whole purpose in life is to serve them. I never did their homework, I didn't feel I had to go to every single one of their

T-ball-soccer-hockey-basketball-volleyball-games, and I certainly never thought it was my job to drive them to or from school.

Sure, I've sat in cold, hard wooden bleachers watching my kid ankle-skate around, and I did my share of coaching swarms of little boys and girls mindlessly chasing a ball and calling it soccer, and I've even been known to chauffeur a child to school on a rainy day, but I never thought I was obligated to do these things. And I don't think it's my job to plan, execute, and live my kids' lives for them. I know that, but still I worry.

And I guess I'm not alone. A week ago I was driving up north with my pal Cesare, who was telling me about his son, who's over in Germany on a college work term. Paolo was doing great, enjoying his job and loving every minute of being a young man in Europe on his own. They talked on Skype regularly, exchanged emails, and generally kept in touch — and still Cesare was anxious. "I miss him and I worry about him," he told me. "I'm not even sure why."

Finally, as a surprise for his wife and his two other children, and partly to allay his anxiety, Cesare flew Paolo home for a week's visit. It was pricey. "And worth every penny," he said. "Once I saw him, once I gave him a hug, I felt okay."

We're a much more "huggy" generation than our parents were, and sometimes it's hard to know who the hugs are for — us or them. Perhaps it's a bit of both.

Rationally, I know that I cannot control everything that is going to happen to my children. I know they may fall ill or have an accident, that they will suffer broken legs and broken hearts, and that I cannot prevent either. I now know that much of who they will become is imprinted at birth and our job is mostly to make sure they are fed and loved and safe.

An old newsroom friend told me when our first child was just a baby, "Everything you can give them you've given by the time they are eight." And yet I think of my own father, who, even in his eighties, would greet me each and every time with the one question that mattered to him most: "How are the kids?"

44

She Fell, Yes. But She Is Not Falling …

April 14, 2012

We did everything we could think of to make sure it did not happen.

When she moved, we made sure the new place had no steps. We installed a safety handle in the bathroom. We complained when the walkway cement slabs leading to her front door shifted and became uneven. We even suggested she think twice about taking a walk on windy days. At just over a hundred pounds, we worried that she might get blown over.

When she decided she'd like to go to Florida in the winter, we arranged every part of the trip. Boarding assistance at both airports, a porter for her suitcase, an airport taxi driver to meet her at the baggage carousel.

We even alerted the front desk of the hotel in St. Pete Beach to be on the lookout for a small, smiling woman arriving on her own. Even with all that in place, we worried. Worried she might trip getting off the plane, or navigating through the airport, or even walking around the town.

But in the end, none of that really mattered.

She fell anyway.

She fell, like my father had fallen before her, doing nothing special or extraordinary or dangerous. At home. Just living.

She fell, like my father, and like most older people, for no reason. My dad tumbled to the floor in the living room, simply making his way to the kitchen. He couldn't explain why. He just fell.

And so it was with my mother, my eighty-five-year-old whirlwind of a mother. She'd travelled thousands of miles to Florida and back on her own, walked the beach every day, gone shopping and out to restaurants and shows, and then came home and fell in her bedroom. "I was coming around the corner of the bed," she said, later. "And maybe I turned too fast and …"

And she fell. Hard. With no time to get her hands out. She just hit the carpeted floor like dead weight. "I heard a thump," she said. "And I thought, Oh Mary, you've done it now."

And when I get the call from my wife and hear the words that we had all hoped we'd never hear, "Your mom fell," my heart trips in my chest and I have to take a deep breath and hold myself still for a moment. Three years ago, when my dad fell, we really had no idea about these things, but now we are all burdened by experience and know all too well what those three small words can bring.

When my father fell on that summer afternoon, he fractured his femur and cracked his hip. He had two surgeries and though he tried and we tried with him, he never stood again. In fact, he never left the hospital. He fell that day and hit the living room floor, but in some ways he just kept falling, down, down, one complication, one bad turn, one piece of bad luck after the other.

Until there was no farther to fall and a few days later we all sat around his bed and let him gently fall one last time into whatever comes after this life.

And so when I arrive at the hospital, I find my brothers, Robert and Joe, and my sister Rosanne, and I can see the worry that knowing brings etched on their faces.

But my mom is good. She's worried but alert and, as she always is, positive. And, of all things, thankful. She's thankful that she was wearing the Lifeline bracelet we bought her and that the EMS folks were there in minutes.

Thankful that she was in the hospital in "the best country in the world," and that they'd given her something for the pain.

And after the operation — she had broken her hip — she is up and stands the very next day. And a day after that, she walks.

And in three days she is well enough to move to rehab. And every doctor and therapist who sees her says the same thing. "She's amazing."

She fell, yes. But she is not falling.

My tiny, smiling, eighty-five-year-old, ever optimistic mother.

Amazing, indeed.

45

Keeping Our Kids "Safe" Inside Is, as Scientists Say, "Stupid"

June 9, 2012

Here's a news flash: scientists announce that kids are not getting enough exercise.

Wow, what's next? Studies show large rocks are heavy? Or researchers discover William Shatner is "weird."

Apparently, in a report ironically titled "Active Healthy Kids Canada," scientists found children scored an "F" for their activity level and their "screen-based sedentary behaviour."

In their annual "report card" released last week, researchers said almost half of Canadian kids got three hours or less of active play per week and spent almost eight hours a day in front of a TV or computer screen of some kind.

Frankly, this shocked me. Some kids are active for three hours a week?

I've seen my kids go seven days without getting off the couch. To them, "active play" includes "finding the remote" and going to the fridge for more snacks.

Recently, when *Diablo III* was released, I didn't see my son for two days. Although he was very busy hacking apart the Lords of Hell outside the Crystal Arch (don't ask — unless you're up for a couple of hours of full nerd overload), I think the only "activity" he experienced was pretty vigorous "mousing" and snapping the tabs on Red Bull cans.

He's not alone. It seems that between smartphones, laptops, iPads, and good old-fashioned TV, a lot of kids rarely leave the house. It was also reported (and I am not making this up) that many parents worry about the safety of letting their kids play outside. The parents have what one scientist called "an excessive fear of the outdoors" — or "extreme stupidity."

If my parents had this fear, they sure did a good job of hiding it. When we were kids down on Stirton Street we spent pretty much every hour of our summer days outside.

Sure, we read comic books and watched *Gilligan's Island*, *Leave It to Beaver*, and other highly educational TV shows, but mostly we went out and hacked around.

My parents, who were busy with the house and taking care of three younger siblings, had one basic message for my older brother Joe and me: "Go outside."

So we played games of British Bulldog or touch football in the park behind our house, or pickup baseball right out on the street. We rode our banana-seat, monkey-bar bikes all over the place, and even went on all-day salamander- and snake-hunting expeditions to the wilds of the "woods" at the mountain's edge.

We'd whip over to Walt's Variety for a Popsicle, or if we were ambitious, we'd walk about a dozen city blocks east on Barton Street to the Dairy Queen.

As the day wore on, we played long games of marbles, flipped hockey cards, smashed shoe-stringed chestnuts together to see whose would be a "kinger," and generally knocked around until somebody's mother would step out onto the back porch and yell, "Dinner!"

We'd all head in for half an hour and then, when supper was over and as the late-afternoon shadows grew longer, we'd play in the streets — usually a game of Kick the Can — and the evening would only end when the street lights came on, the universal curfew for little kids.

Maybe a lot of children today are inside slaying virtual dragons for hours on end, but I'm happy to say that where I live the street is filled with kids playing road hockey. Every day after school, Wesley, Solomon, Jack, Graham, Rafael, and a few others set up their net. One brave boy straps on the goalie pads and the rest grab their sticks and do their best impression of the Stanley Cup finals without the fighting and the beer commercials.

And they go and go and go; the clacking and slapping of their sticks and the shouts of "Car!" and "He scores!" become the soundtrack of the street.

The only safety issue is the occasional skinned knee, and the only sedentary thing is me, sitting watching the scene from my front porch. Maybe they're too young for *Diablo* or maybe their parents won't let them on the computer. But whatever the case, there they are, day after day, playing on the road. Actually outside.

Imagine.

46

Cottaging by the (Wet) Seat of My Pants

July 7, 2012

For many Canadians, July is a popular vacation time, which means many people are at work doing nothing while their boss fights traffic up to his fancy-pants cottage.

When you get tired of killing time at your desk surfing the Internet — because, really, how many pictures of Maria Sharapova can anyone look at? — it's probably time for you to get away from the high-stress office environment and go on vacation.

For those lucky enough to get up to a cottage — preferably not with your boss — there are a host of things you can do, usually known as "traditional cottage activities" or "torture."

If you end up in the Muskoka region, remember to wear plaid shorts and a pastel-coloured polo shirt; otherwise you'll be stopped by local police and politely asked what you are doing around here and if you "need directions to Bobcaygeon."

Once you are at the cottage, it will only be a matter of minutes before your host wants to take you out in the boat for a "lake tour." This is code for buzzing around gawking at the "cottages" of millionaires. These humble shacks are big enough to host a Rotary convention and have all the rustic charm of a Marriott hotel, but with more helipads.

After you've spent an hour or so finding out what your broker actually did with your RRSP money ("Hey, sorry about your retirement, but it's expensive running six Sea-Doos and a new Donzi!"), you return to the cottage for drinks and a couple hours of deep self-pity. You may also want to keep a watchful eye on your wife for any hint of a medical condition known as "Wow, how can I find a way to dump this loser and hook up with Kurt Russell?"

In other parts of cottage country, the traditional boat trip takes on various and equally painful forms. On Lake Erie, your host will convince you that it's fun to spend several hours fighting a two-foot chop to motor past the natural beauty of the hydro station on your way to Port Dover, a quaint lakeside spot where you can get a great hot dog while listening to the sound of about a thousand Harley-Davidsons. I know because I've been the host that did this.

If you head to the picturesque shores of Georgian Bay, prepare yourself for the mandatory boat ride, which is quite an ordeal because everything there is "about an hour away" — even the cottage swim raft. After you've spent several hours packing and checking the sky (ho-ho, that could be quite a storm brewing!), you head out.

Georgian Bay is roughly the size of Arizona but with more water and probably more Democrats. The bay is known for its stunning vistas and the charming fact that it is home to thousands of gigantic rocks sitting just below the water's surface, ever ready to tear off the entire bottom off your boat.

So the hour-long ride is a delightful blend of high-speed, spine-crunching wave slams offset by the constant threat of immediate death. Because of motor noise, these trips are also known for their sparkling conversation, which goes like this:

Captain (pointing): "Over there is rodlah blubgabble."

Me: "Wow."

After what seems like only a couple of days, you reach the island. The people who can still walk climb out of the boat onto a slime-covered shoal designed to make anyone over the age of twenty flip into the air and land on their keister. The "island" is a chunk of pink granite that is home to a couple of scrubby dwarf pines. It's actually stunning and would make for a great painting, but it's a less-than-perfect picnic spot.

After we open a beer, let the dogs run around, and relieve ourselves behind the lone pine tree, we find an official government notice that reads: "Two-hour maximum visit. No alcohol. No dogs. No peeing."

We head back to the boat. Actually, I enjoy a good ride over open water, but I'm always happy to get back to the cottage deck. The drinks are wet, the seats are dry, and you can exceed the two-hour maximum.

47

The Journey Is Half the Fun. Isn't It?

August 18, 2012

Summer is the time of wonderful family vacations.

Okay, how about just family vacations.

You may be heading off to an interesting city — or Edmonton — or perhaps to a pleasant campground or cottage in Ontario's vast north just beyond Canada's Wonderland.

Either way, the trip will involve a long car drive. This was always a fun and exciting part of our family vacations.

Even the packing was exciting. Exciting because, as kids, we lived in an almost constant state of terror that during the tension-filled loading of the car, the top of my father's head might blow off.

My dad would spend hours trying to jam a week's supplies for a family of seven into the trunk of a regular four-door sedan. To accomplish this, he used a lot of brute force and a series of words in both English and Italian that rarely make it into the Queen's annual address to Parliament.

Once this packing was done — usually about two hours after scheduled departure time — we would pack seven of us into the Pontiac Laurentian. I don't know how we all actually fit, but I have a vague memory of my screaming brother Robert holding on to the roof rack all the way up Highway 6.

Once everything and everyone was loaded in, we would merrily head off on vacation. Often we would get as much as a full city block from home before someone would say, "Did we remember to bring the (fill any word you like in here)? Sometimes, this word included the name of a member of the family. We would drive back around the block, watching my dad's face go from just plain red to a kind of eggplant-like hue, to pick up whatever — or whomever — we had left behind. We would repeat this two or three times just to add to the festive spirit of the trip.

Finally, we would get on the road for our three-hour-plus ride up to Sauble Beach. It took this long because about every twelve minutes one of five kids would need to pee. My dad found our asynchronous bladders quite amusing and he would vigorously pound the steering wheel each time we requested a stop. My mom would try to lighten the strain of the trip — I'm pretty sure we were actually sitting ON TOP of one another — with games and songs. We'd play I Spy or other word games, and my mom knew dozens of big band songs and show tunes and we'd all sing along.

When my father would sit up and death-grip the steering wheel to pull out to pass and then floor the over-packed car, with seemingly no discernible increase in speed, she'd break into a rousing rendition of "Oklahoma!" to cover the screaming.

Despite it all, we had fun on the road — the journey as much a part of the holiday as the cottaging. Not today. Last week, my wife and I joined her sister and husband on the drive to a cottage weekend with friends. I sat up front with my brother-in-law Woody and the women took over the rest of the van.

The first part of the trip was a lively exchange of cellphone rings and the sound of people tapping text messages. Then we had the delightful opportunity to listen to one side of cellphone calls to the office that were almost as interesting as the Weather Channel but with no pictures.

Then the women decided they'd like to watch something on the inboard DVD system. They felt it would be "really great for all of us" if they watched a dozen episodes of *Downton Abbey* at full volume. Of course, Woody and I cannot see anything and the sound is up so high that we can't talk over all the, "Good God, man, it's war with Germany! We've got to do something. Shall I fetch the gin for you?"

Imagine being blindfolded and forced to listen to a hundred episodes of *Upstairs Downstairs* with a bit of car sickness thrown in for fun and you've got the picture.

Me, I'll take the crowded Pontiac anytime.

48

Missing Matt

September 15, 2012

It started about midsummer.

My wife and I would be sitting at the dining room table after dinner and she would be become quiet, her expression somewhere between confusion and concern.

"Are you okay?" I'd ask.

The words seemed to act like a key, and a door would open and with that her face would collapse, tears streaming down her cheeks.

"I've never felt like this before," she said. "I don't know what's wrong with me."

"It's okay," I'd say, feeling helpless, like most men, in the face of tears.

I think we both knew what was wrong in some way, though like a lot of these things, it had come upon her slowly and incrementally, like a siren in the distance that grows louder and louder until it's blaring in your ears.

It started with a rare phone call from our middle child, Matthew, who has been travelling in the U.K. and Europe. It was spring and Matt had by then spent a year away from home, working in England and Scotland, hiking in the Highlands, camel riding in Morocco, and just generally doing what young men do on their first foray from home. He sounded oddly tentative, explaining that he was done with Edinburgh; the work was hard, the wages low, and it seemed like a good time to go.

"I'm thinking of coming back to Canada," he said, and my wife's face lit up with the prospect of getting her baby boy back. "I think I might take some time and explore Canada, like I did the U.K.," he said.

"Oh, yeah," I said, "and where do you think you'll start?"

"Well, I was thinking Saskatchewan. There's lots of work there."

"Uh-huh. And that pretty young woman who is beside you in all the Facebook photos, where might she be from?" I asked.

"Saskatchewan. Saskatoon actually," he said.

Of course.

So one journey had led to another journey — this one of the heart. "You'll come home first?" we asked hopefully.

"No," he said, a hint of apology in his voice. He would fly directly to Calgary, where his friend Laura would meet him.

And that's what he did, and the idea that he was jetting above us and past us began to settle somewhere into my wife's consciousness.

It didn't help that he didn't call. At least, it didn't help me. Each day, my wife would wonder out loud how Matt was doing. Why we hadn't heard from him, and each day I would gently explain that he was fine and living his life and not thinking that he had to "check in."

And so she would let a few days go by, but then, overwhelmed by her desire to connect, she would get on the computer and repeatedly try to Skype him.

When he finally answered, we had a nice, long catch-up call, meeting Laura (at least electronically), who was sitting beside him on the couch. He was happy, looking forward to work — probably construction — and enjoying Saskatchewan, visiting Laura's relatives, getting to know Saskatoon. He was not travelling now. He was living.

It was after that call, I think, that things changed. Several realities that we had perhaps both held at bay became clear: Matt was not coming home anytime soon.

And perhaps, more importantly, when he did come home, he would no longer, and would never again, be the boy who had left a short year ago. That boy was gone, replaced by the still smiling, still gentle young man on our computer screen.

That truth, however simple, and of course inevitable, made my wife weep. Not for a few minutes or even several hours, but for days. And then one evening, with sudden tears again running down her cheeks, she said, "I know what it is, what I'm feeling. It's a sense of loss."

And we came to understand together something my father had tried once long ago to express to me: that for parents, there is but a blink between the baby and the boy and then a brief moment between the boy and the man.

That, as we had so often told our children, growing up is hard. Hard for them.

And, as we now know, perhaps even harder for us.

49

The (Old) Boys Decide to Hit the Town …

October 27, 2012

A couple of my friends recently decided it would be a good idea to have a "boys' night out." For the purposes of this article and to avoid embarrassment, I will call them Mike and Adriaan. (Their actual names are Mike and Adriaan.) What follows is a series of emails we exchanged to organize the evening. Some of the details have been changed to make me look better.

> Subject: Guys' Get-Together
> Hello Gentlemen, it's October and high time the three of us got out for some well-deserved male recreation! Let's set a date.
> — Mike

> Sounds great! I'm in, but I have some travel for work. I'm tied up October 15 through 20 and then from the 29th to the end of the month. And a little bit into November. But other than that: hoo-haa! Let's go.
> — Adriaan

> I am out of the office. If this is important, wait a couple of days and email me again.
> — Paul

Greetings sturdy lads! Have not heard from Paul, but fully loaded for ripping up the proverbial town! Once we find a few days where Adriaan is not out of town, shall we hit a series of night clubs and dance bars? Flaming shooters anyone? We can all crash at our house. I'm stoked!

— Mike

Sorry, finally checked my email. Your messages marked "PartyTime" went straight into my Spam Account along with "Make $$$ from Home!" and "Bigger Penis? You Bet!" I'm good to go, just need to check with my wife on what dates we are committed to either a boring fundraiser or a boring dinner. Will be in touch, brothers!

— Paul

Fellow Revellers! What say ye? Still waiting on you Benny! You think we can set a date before the year is up? BTW, should I book a limo?

— Mike

I'm still good to go Mike. But not really sure about the whole "nightclub" thing. I haven't danced since my nephew's wedding in '08 and I pulled a hamstring pretty bad during the Chicken Dance. Plus my sciatica's been acting up lately. I'm up for full revelling, but can we do it mostly seated?

— Adriaan

Fellow Pirates! We are booked! Nov. 9th. Brace yourselves!

— Mike

Okay boys. Caught up with you. The 9th is good. Mike, why don't you come this way? Skip the limo and we can party here in the Hammer. And I'm pretty much on a Non-Shooter Diet since a somewhat unfortunate incident at a neighbour's home where after several rounds of tequila I "accidentally" backed their barbecue into the pool — with the steaks still on it. Perhaps a few ales instead?

— Paul

Ahoy Mates! Slight change of departure dates. I forgot the 9th is my mom's 85th birthday. Let's reschedule. Sorry bros.

— Mike

Whew! I was just about to tell you guys I misread the calendar (you know October, November, they all look alike) ... we're hosting a dinner party the 9th. Boys' Booze-Up Re-sked looks good to me!

— Paul

Okay. I have double-checked work and home and Nov. 16th looks good. I usually catch a quick nap on Friday after work, so can we start this party up about 8 p.m.?

— Adriaan

Sure Adriaan. Do you want me to bring a little blanket for you for the car ride? Okay, Okay, have your nap, but steel yourself lads for a Night of Excess! I'm bringing a fistful of hand-rolled Cubans and a bottle of Jack Daniel's. We're Rat Packing, boys!

— Mike

All right Mike! We are ready for take off, Houston! Just one thing. Cigars have an interesting medical effect on me. They make me turn green and then shortly thereafter, everyone around me is covered in vomit. Otherwise, Let's rock!

— Paul

Okay. We can grab a beer at the local pub and I've booked a table at our favourite steak house. That way, we can walk.

— Adriaan

Great A. My plantar fasciitis is killing me. A short walk and a steak sound right. This might be blasphemy but, you know, drinks and a nice dinner — maybe we should invite the wives?

— Paul

Really? Oh hell, all right. I'll see if she's free.

— Mike

I'll check my calendar.

— Adriaan

I am out of the office. If this is important, wait a couple of days and email me again.

— Paul

140-Character Witticisms

November 10, 2012

I followed the U.S. presidential election extremely closely on Tuesday evening, except for the periods where I was asleep.

In fact, I paid a lot of attention to the whole campaign, including the crazy claims in the vicious attack ads like: "ObamaCare has Death Panels" and "Romney thinks 47 percent of Americans are leeches." Oh wait, that last one is kinda true.

I decided that the best way to watch the election night results was to actually WATCH the election night results. I decided not to use social media or be on Facebook or Twitter. For those of you who do not know what Facebook is, I hope that you are feeling better after your coma. And for people unfamiliar with Twitter, well, good for you! Keep up the good work.

I decided all this because a couple weeks ago I tried using Twitter while watching the U.S. presidential debates. Here's what I found out.

First, even if you think you are tweeting and watching the debates, you are not. You are doing either, but not both. It's a lot like reading the newspaper at breakfast and listening to your wife. You think you are doing both, but she knows you're not. And here's an unpleasant reality: you are doing neither particularly well.

This is what happens.

You are watching the debates. Romney says something you think might be funny. You look down at your iPad and try to type something witty about "binders full of women." You are moderately successful: "Wow, women in binders — that's gotta be claustrophobic!"

By the time you look up, you realize the debate has moved on. Jeez, what are they talking about now? Jobs? Detroit? Who said "Tesla?" What did I miss?

You glance back at Twitter. Now everyone is talking about "going home to cook dinner at 5:00 p.m." but you didn't hear Mitt because you were too busy typing a funny remark about something else he said earlier.

So you start to listen to the debate again, but you keep glancing back at your Twitter feed, so it's tough to follow.

As you read the Twitter feed, you realize everyone is kind of doing the same thing: they're typing quips as fast as they can. It's like a virtual cocktail party with about two hundred Oscar Wilde wannabes. Everyone seems to be frantically trying to "out-wit" each other. It's literally a steady stream of one-liners, one-upmanship, and one wonders, What's the point?

I follow some pretty smart, informed folks, but even the brightest people are not always enlightening or amusing in 140 characters at light speed.

I'll bet Oscar Wilde probably mulled over his witticisms, crafting them at home and then "spontaneously" lobbing them out at parties. Not so with Twitter. People are typing as fast as they can think, and frankly, sometimes faster. And that's not factoring wine with dinner or beers after work.

Intelligent discourse? Trenchant commentary? A virtual conversation? I don't think so. Here are some real samples:

"I hate it when politicians want to run the government like a company. Have you ever been a customer at Walmart? No thanks."

"If you don't understand the differences between these two candidates by now, I lovingly call you a moron."

"I have to admit they're both pretty handsome. I'm waiting for the swimsuit competition to decide."

"Mitt Romney is giving me a headache."

"Twenty dollars says Romney can't point to Syria on a map."

So, some of this is funny, some of it is obvious, and some of it is just inane. But even when it's funny, it's a bit like trying to listen to a political speech while a team of stand-up comedians riff off it IN YOUR LIVING ROOM. Try concentrating while that's going on.

But then again, who's concentrating anyway? How can you focus on anything really when you're constantly interrupting yourself to answer email, check your cellphone, send texts, and tweet all day?

I can't even concentrate on writing this…. Sorry, what was I saying? I just took a break to tweet that I'm writing this piece.

In fact, never mind, I'll just boil the whole thing down to 140 characters later.

51

Old Underwear Is No Accident

November 24, 2012

Recently, I ventured out to buy some new underwear.

This is not usually very high on my Fun Things to Do on the Weekend list, but after months of delay, I had no choice.

My suite of underwear was in bad shape — loose, baggy, and in many cases, ventilated. Putting them on some mornings, I would be met with "that look" from my wife.

"You're going to wear THOSE to work?"

"Why not? I'm not really planning on anyone seeing them today," I say. "Underwear Day at the office is next week."

"Funny," she says. "Even if no one sees them, they are still a disgrace."

This, of course, makes no sense to most men. We barely care what people think of the clothing they CAN see. You think a guy who wears sweatpants and a Leafs jersey to a wedding (hey, it's his BEST Leafs jersey) cares about the exact state of his boxers? This is a woman thing and when I hear it, I can't help but recall my mother's voice from our childhood.

"Did you put on fresh underwear?" she'd ask me and my brothers at the breakfast table. "You never know when you are going to be in an accident."

This perplexed me as a ten-year-old and still does. First, she made an accident sound like it was some kind of an important and possibly good event. Like, "Gee, I might get whacked by a truck on my way to school — I should put on a nicer shirt." But mostly, I didn't get it because boys don't worry about much about their underwear in general, and even less so during an auto wreck.

I figure if I'm in a terrible car accident, pretty much the last thing I'm going to care about is how my underwear looks.

And what's really going to happen anyway? They wheel you into the hospital ER on a stretcher, doctors and nurses running alongside.

Doctor: "Okay, car accident victim here. Compound fracture of the femur. Cracked ribs. Multiple contusions. Let's prep for surgery. Stat!"

Nurse: "Yes, doctor." (She scissors off your jeans.)

Doctor: "Whoa! Hold up here. Take a look at those undies. Multiple holes. Saggy waistband. I'm not sure I can proceed."

Nurse: "What's wrong with people? I can't work like this."

Nonetheless, my brothers and I did put on clean underwear every day, just so my mom wouldn't be embarrassed.

Old habits die hard and I have to admit that when I leave in the morning, I worry a bit that I may have some kind of Public Underwear Incident (don't ask) and won't be properly attired.

So I head out to buy new undergarments. I quickly find out this is not as simple as it seems. Wander into The Bay and you'll immediately notice that the men's underwear section is the size of a football field. There have to be four hundred kinds of underwear to choose from. I remember when you had a vast range of choice between Stanfield's and McGregor all the way to McGregor and Stanfield's.

And they came in an amazing array of styles. Well, okay, two exactly: boxers or briefs. So, mathematically, even with every possible combination (No, I cannot figure that out. Journalists are prevented from "doing math" by national law), you could basically make your underwear-buying decision in five seconds. Actually, less. If you were under fifty years of age: briefs. Over fifty: boxers.

Colour was even easier. You could choose white, white, or white.

Today, the whole underwear scene is a decision-making nightmare. Here are just some of the styles of underwear you can buy — and I'm not making this up. There is the classic brief (the kind you wore as a kid or "tighty-whiteys"), woven boxer, athletic boxer, cotton-knit boxer, cotton-stretch trunk, boxer brief, fitted boxer, colour fitted boxer, regular rise brief, loose boxer, and something called classic-fit loose boxer. I'm not sure what goes into making underwear "classic," but whatever it is, it adds ten dollars to the price.

After an hour, I wandered out confused — and without any new underwear.

I think I'll just do what all guys who need underwear do — wait for Christmas.

52

Our New Christmas: Different, but in Many Ways the Same

December 22, 2012

Christmas has changed.

No, scratch that. Our Christmas has changed.

For years, Christmas Day was a tightly choreographed set of events beginning when our three kids woke up at dawn. They would have sprung out of their beds even earlier, but we drew the line if it was still dark out. Our excuse to them was that they might frighten away Santa and the reindeer doing their end-of-the-night deliveries. That usually worked.

We'd allow them to open a couple of gifts (or maybe three or four) and then we'd all dress up and head off to Christmas morning mass.

It was sometimes a struggle to manage three young kids in a hot, standing-room-only church (we never got there early, ever) but as long as the homily was not too long, we survived.

Then it was home for a moment and up to my parents' house for *pranzo*, an elaborate lunch that would stretch lazily through multiple courses and into the early evening.

Sometimes the children would nap, sometimes we would nap, but by five o'clock, we'd have to regroup to — I know this was crazy — drive over to my in-laws' home and eat another full Christmas dinner. Even in the haze of nostalgia, I'd be lying if I didn't admit that sometimes as the evening wore on there were tantrums and tears — and the kids behaved pretty badly, too.

Finally, we'd bundle them up and take them home, let them play a little longer with their new toys and then put them to bed. It was always fun, but a bit of a blur and we'd often take a moment to sit on the couch, eat one more chocolate or sip on a small brandy, and then, as exhausted as the children, go to bed.

For a few years we tried the midnight mass thing, but the kids got older and began to make their own choices and soon we simply stopped going to Christmas mass altogether. Other things changed, too. Our own families got bigger and it just became impractical to have two full dinners in one day every year. As well, though my mom and mother-in-law are alive and healthy, they are both well into their eighties and it's clearly our time to cook for them. So, now the kids take turns hosting the big dinner, and with that we have ended some traditions and started others.

There have been other changes as well. My father is gone and so is my father-in-law. And last year, for the first time ever, our middle child, Matthew, was not home for Christmas. He was away travelling in Europe and we all missed him at the table.

I accept these changes, but in many ways I cling to the past. I like to prepare a big fish dinner on Christmas Eve, rekindling a family tradition and a centuries-old Italian custom — the Feast of the Seven Fishes. On Christmas morning, I like coffee and panettone, a sweet Italian fruit bread that was a childhood Christmas treat, and I still enjoy watching *White Christmas*, but I'm usually on the couch alone because the kids find it hokey and slow.

I like Christmas music, at least in the week before the 25th, and I like walking in our neighbourhood at night and seeing the houses lit up against winter's gloom.

Perhaps it's age, but each year I care less and less about presents and more and more about the people around me. And this year, I look forward to what will be the best present of all. Matthew is coming home. He left on May 10, 2011, and I have not seen my twenty-year-old son for more than a year and a half.

When he comes through our door I will hold him in my arms and feel his unshaven cheek against my face and I will hug him hard and for too long and I will be happy.

So perhaps things are not so different. All of our children will be at the table again and our home will be warm and bright. We will sit together and tell stories. We will laugh a lot and probably cry a little. And it will be our Christmas.

53

A Low-Res Year

January 5, 2013

Over the holidays we went to a cottage for a couple of days and I made the mistake of picking up an *O* magazine.

For those of you who have been lost at sea for several years — and for all men — *O* is short for *The Oprah Magazine*, a monthly put out by Oprah Winfrey that features Oprah on every cover, an editor's note from Oprah, articles about many serious issues like Oprah's diet, Oprah's homes, and other things you didn't care about that concern Oprah.

Other than the voluminous amount of Oprah information in every issue, what you cannot fail to notice is that the entire magazine is about self-improvement. On virtually every page there is advice on how to eat better, sleep sounder, run faster, get smarter, be slimmer, get taller, and finally, be more like Oprah.

And this time of year, the same thing goes for every newspaper you look at and every website you visit. They're all filled with articles with titles like "You in Review," in which you painfully go over your failed promises, missed opportunities, and abandoned projects of 2012.

And they wonder why people drink on New Year's Eve?

So, in honour of slackers, procrastinators, and half-milers everywhere (I actually belong to a Slackers, Procrastinators, and Half-Milers Club, but no one ever makes the meetings), here is a New Year's list of Things You DON'T Have to Do in 2013:

You Don't Have to Tweet More (or at all). Why? Do you really think that people all over the world are glued to their computer screens waiting for you to type, "Mmmm, just ate a nice sandwich"? A great many people tweeting end up confirming they are idiots (Donald Trump); being fined (all professional athletes); being fired (too many names to list, but a lot of journalists, who should know better); and boring everyone to death (almost everyone). Let's face it, once the Holy Pontiff himself claims to be on Twitter, I'd say any "cool factor" it once had has pretty much passed.

You Don't Have to Eat More Fruit. Why? Because we now know that fruit is dangerous. That's because scientists have discovered that apples and pineapples are actually "nutritional stealth bombers" — clever delivery systems for something called "fructose" which is basically "sucrose" disguised as a banana. Nutritionally, it's like arsenic only sweeter.

You Don't Have to Exercise a Lot. This year, extremely smart scientists, many of whom were employed by the people who bring you Twinkies, announced that "extreme exercise" could cause long-term damage to your heart. This was a virtual "get out of jail free card" for everyone who needs a new excuse NOT to exercise. The key of course is how to define "excessive exercise." I like to put the bar at anything beyond "getting up for the remote" and "taking out the garbage" as potentially dangerous.

You Don't Have to See a Counsellor, Life Coach, or Psychiatrist. Well, maybe you do. That's because with the latest changes to the DSM — the diagnostic bible for psychologists and psychiatrists — EVERYTHING that can happen to you is a disorder or a disease. Forget where you put your keys? You've got "Minor Neurocognitive Disorder." Eat too may burritos, pizzas, and wings? No, you're not in a hockey beer league; you've got "Binge Eating Disorder." Worried about everyday things like your kids, your job, and your finances? You don't have an overdue Visa bill, you've got "Generalized Anxiety Disorder"! So, now that virtually every living person on the planet has a mental disorder, I think we can all relax and have a sandwich.

Finally, all of this "not doing things" can be pretty daunting, so don't try to not do everything all at once. Rome wasn't unbuilt in a day. Take it one day at a time. Experts say that it's easy to slip on your New Year's non-resolutions and then give up. So, remember, you will slide a bit, it's only human — perhaps you catch yourself exercising one day or tweeting — well, don't despair, you can just regroup and not do anything the next day! It's tough work, but somebody has to not do it.

54

And These Are My Children ...
Venti, Grande, and Tall

March 2, 2013

Lately, I've been seeing a lot of stories about how young people are under-employed in Canada. Many of them with completed university degrees are working in jobs that don't make any use of the intellectual skills they have developed — as baristas, for example, or politicians.

For those of you who do not have a child who is a university graduate or have never set foot in a Starbucks, please let me have your bank account. No, I mean, you may not know what a barista is. *Barista* is the Italian word for bartender and usually refers to the man or woman behind the bar at an espresso shop. There, the person applies their full university-gained knowledge of ancient civilizations or the modern British novel to pouring really hot milk into coffee and making a butterfly in the foam.

Starbucks says baristas "create uplifting experience for the people who visit our stores and make perfect beverages — one drink and one person at a time."

Oddly, the same thing has happened to me.

I, too, have a university education (though, I have had several calls from McMaster about "wanting their degree back" but I have ignored them) and in the past month I've been spending a lot of my free time making coffee for one person at a time. And not getting paid for it.

Let me explain.

For some time now (about two decades, but who's counting?) I've wanted an espresso coffee machine. The problem is good ones are not cheap and I've never quite been able to find the right moment to get one because other small things — like groceries and heat — have got in the way. Every Christmas and birthday, I've hinted that an espresso machine might be a nice gift, but the closest I've come is a pair of coffee-coloured socks.

And then I had a revelation. I realized that God was speaking directly to me and telling me to run for prime minister. Just kidding. The revelation was an envelope in the mail, buried among the pizza flyers and real estate agent cards exhorting me to sell my home (which is actually a good combination because if we did that we'd probably be living in a pizza box).

It was a letter telling me how many reward miles I had built up with a company we'll call Fair Miles so that no one will recognize the real company I'm talking about. Fair Miles informed me that after more than ten years of handing over their blue-and-white card so that they could track my every purchase and report it to my wife, I had actually accumulated a significant number of Fair Miles Reward Miles. I could either use these miles for a fabulous one-way flight to Sault Ste. Marie (but only when the seats are available — usually mid-January) or I could redeem them for household appliances or electronics.

It was a tough call, but I opted for the latter. I went online, found a wonderful stainless steel beauty of an espresso machine, and ordered it! I just clicked on the machine I wanted and presto! — a few days later, a big box arrived at my door and a few hours later I was in coffee heaven. Or so I thought.

At first it was fun, tamping down the coffee, shooting up espressos and frothing the milk. Everyone loved the coffees and I was an instant barista star without having to wear a funny uniform and say things like "Grande or super grande?" to anyone. I loved it.

But within days, things began to go off the rails. In the morning now, my daughter does not even bother getting out of bed before yelling out: "Daaa-aad! I'd like a double-shot vanilla latte, skinny, no sugar, extra hot and extra foam. Pronto! Pleeeeeease!"

The first hour of my mornings is now devoted to filling coffee orders in my kitchen. The only difference between me and most coffee shop baristas is thirty years, twenty pounds, and a fist full of tips. After a busy morning of barista work, I really need a break and a nice cup of coffee. Now, I do what most people do.

Head to Tim Hortons.

55

Love Beyond Our Imperfections

March 30, 2013

A little more than a week ago, the mother of one of our very good friends died.

Her death was unexpected, as much as a death at eighty-five years of age can be unexpected.

It was, like the deaths of many old people, neither a shock nor a tragedy. She had complained of leg pain, gone to the hospital, and the next day a blood clot moved through her body to her heart or her head and killed her. Though in a retirement home, she had been up to that point of relatively sound body and mind. And like most of us, my friend and her family saw the quick and uncomplicated death, though sad, as something of a blessing.

On the weekend, there was a small celebration of this woman's life. There was a simple, private burial of her ashes at Holy Sepulchre Cemetery, where my friend and her three siblings stood in the spring sunshine and said their goodbyes.

At the graveside where her father was buried, my friend gave her mother a brief eulogy from neatly typed notes that she later handed me and gave me the privilege of reading.

She did a good job with a difficult task and there was something in her words when I first read them that struck me, but that I could not quite identify.

Her mother's life had not been easy and my friend was open and honest that their relationship had been a complicated and not always happy one. She acknowledged the complexity of her mother's sometimes troubled life and then spoke about her in earlier and happier times. About her youthful zest for living and her beauty. She talked about the gifts her mother had given her, gifts that had in central ways shaped her life.

She spoke about her mother's love of nature, her appreciation of Canada's natural beauty, and her simple affection for fishing. She talked about the long afternoons they had spent with their lines in the water, not catching much of anything, but just enjoying the silent reflection that comes when you are calm in yourself and doing something you like. She talked about how she had passed that love of fishing on to her own daughter and sons.

She told the people standing solemnly in the cool, spring air about her mother's talent for knitting and crocheting, an art she herself had never mastered and now likely never would.

She talked about her mother's love of food, about her respect and gratitude for the bounty of the earth. She recalled childhood memories of autumn days spent chopping basketfuls of vegetables and of canning tomatoes and beets and peppers until the jars lined the basement shelves.

She spoke of how that love of cooking and baking had stayed with her, a lifelong affair with food and all that it can do to heal and draw people together.

And when she was done, they set down the urn filled with her mother's ashes and she and her siblings stood by the graveside for a time. Then they filed back to their cars and reconvened at her home for some lunch, drinks, and conversation.

There, we joined them and stood around, chatted and watched as old photos filled with smiling faces, scenes of brides and grooms and babies and, well, life, clicked along on the TV screen — a looping slideshow of a life lived flickering by on a Saturday afternoon.

I left a few hours later and walked through the waning afternoon light to my home. I slipped off my jacket and loosened my tie and lay down on the couch and my mind filled with all that I had seen and heard.

And I thought about being a parent and I knew that though I have tried to do my best for my children as her mother had, I have made mistakes at times, fallen short. And that, despite my honest efforts and best intentions, I would likely, through circumstance and flaws of character, fall short again. I thought that all of us, our parents and us as parents — all of us — are flawed.

And I hoped that my children would in time come to understand this and, like my friend, have the maturity to accept it and the grace to forgive.

56

The Penny Drops on Mother's Day

May 25, 2013

A couple weeks ago, on Mother's Day, my wife woke up to, well … nothing.

No bouquet of flowers. No strawberries and cream and hot espresso on a tray. Not even a large Tim Hortons and a Dutchie. Nothing.

Our eldest child, James, was in the basement sleeping or up early reading, but either way the chances of him remembering it was Mother's Day were about as good as him remembering to take out the recycling that night. Near zero.

Our middle child, Matthew, was in Saskatoon and likely fast asleep. My wife had made what is known as "Pre-emptive Mother's Day Anti-Disappointment Contact" the day before by calling and gently reminding Matt that Mother's Day was imminent. He assured her that he would have called Sunday (likely, his girlfriend would have reminded him) and all was well.

And Ella, our sixteen-year-old daughter, was where teenagers are on Sunday morning — asleep open-mouthed in a tangle of sheets and pillows.

My wife feels some of the situation in our home is my fault, and I have to reluctantly admit she's right.

I grew up with a father who had a universal disdain for what he called "phony celebrations," claiming they were invented by greeting card companies and retail merchants. He treated all these "holidays" and particularly Father's Day the same way, grudgingly sitting down to a nice dinner and accepting our gifts of bad ties and cheap aftershave, but complaining throughout. Under the sarcasm was his real feeling, that what counted was not how you treated your mother on Mother's Day, but how you treated her every day. And he lived that.

My grandmother lived in our home from the moment my parents were married and throughout our entire childhoods. Later, when her health failed, my dad moved her into a retirement home and visited regularly despite the demands of commuting, a challenging job, and five kids. Once, during the drive to visit her, I asked him, with all the tact of a teenager, how he had "put up" with having his mother living with him his entire adult life. He looked at me and said simply, "She's my mother." I thought of my own mother, and understood.

So, on Sunday morning, I called my mom, wished her a happy Mother's Day, and invited her to dinner. Out of pity, I made my wife a nice hot latte and some toast and we got on with the day. She went out and bought my mom a lovely plant that later would make me look like a good son.

As the day wore on, I began to worry a bit. I gently reminded the kids that Nonna would be coming for dinner because, you know, it's MOTHER'S DAY. As usual, James disappeared into the basement and Ella retired to her room for the rest of the afternoon.

I picked up my mom, we had a nice dinner together, and just when I thought all was lost, Ella came to the table with a loosely wrapped package. "This is for you," she said and handed it to her mother.

Inside was a cream-coloured sheet of watercolour paper on which Ella had meticulously painted a bouquet of flowers.

"This is lovely," said my wife.

"Turn it over," said Ella.

On the back, she found a message carefully scribed in black ink. My wife began to read the words aloud, but could not finish.

Happy Mother's Day, Mom.

Thank you for supporting me.

Thank you for caring for me when I'm sad.

Thank you for taking care of me when I'm sick.

Thank you for being patient when I'm difficult.

Thank you for looking out for me.

Thank you for paying for my useless wants.
Thank you for driving me around.
Thank you for understanding me.
Thank you for teaching me what it means to be a wonderful woman.
Thank you for teaching me to care for others.
Thank you for teaching me to always fight for what I believe in.
Thank you for being my Mother.
I love you,
Ella

"That's beautiful," she said, tears streaming down her face.
I think that beat breakfast in bed.

57

Giving a Whole New Meaning to "Couch Surfing"

August 3, 2013

Sometime during the summer, I lost our house.

I don't mean I couldn't find the house. Most days I am perfectly capable of finding my house, and that includes evenings, unless I've been over to my neighbour Dave's for what he calls "an eensy-teensy martini" before dinner. Then I have been known to wander up and down the street a while before settling on my own address.

No, I mean I somehow lost control of my house this summer. The whole thing reminded me a bit of the character in an Ernest Hemingway (dead American author famous for being in a Woody Allen movie) novel who is asked, "How did you go bankrupt?" And he says, "Two ways. Gradually, then suddenly."

That's how I felt. First, our son Matthew came home from Saskatchewan with his girlfriend, Laura, so they took over the upstairs spare room. No problem. Then our basement started to leak. I'm not talking about a bit of extra humidity, or some moist walls, or even the usual trickle of water after a giant rainstorm. I'm talking about a "Wow-that-looks-like-a-trout-pond" kind of leak.

For a while James, who has his bedroom in the basement, managed by getting up every two hours to Shop-Vac the water up. But when I found him in bed one morning wearing a life jacket, I knew things had gone too far. I told my wife we needed to take immediate action in the basement for James's safety. I suggested we buy him an inflatable dinghy in which to sleep. "They're soft and they float," I said.

"Right," she said, contemptuously. "Forget the dinghy. He's coming upstairs immediately. Think of the mould down there."

"Mould? What's wrong with a little mould?" I said. "Penicillin is made from mould. He could be the healthiest person in the house."

This argument did not work, and soon James was carrying his stuff over a small makeshift bridge he had constructed over the water. Thankfully, he left behind the bottles, cans, chip bags, and pizza boxes that make up his bedroom "decor," but he appeared to be hauling about four thousand pounds of computer equipment up the stairs.

"I'm confused," I said to my wife. "If Matt is in the guest room and Ella has her room, where is James going to sleep?" My wife just smiled at me.

As I packed my stuff into the car, I realized that somehow I had been kicked out of my own home. For the next few weeks, we would split our time between the cottage and my sister and brother-in-law's place while the basement was repaired. This sounded okay for about twelve seconds and then it hit me.

"You mean we're leaving the home to our three kids?" I said in a panic. "Are you insane? It'll be *Animal House* in a week. In two weeks, it'll look like *World War Z*!"

"Paul, relax," she said. "The kids are fine. They'll take care of the house and it will be a nice chance for them to bond without us around."

After a few days at the cottage, I couldn't take it any longer so I drove home to check on the house. On the front porch, I found James quietly studying, his textbooks piled on chairs around him. In the kitchen, I found Laura cheerfully loading the dishwasher. In the basement, I found Matthew tearing out wet drywall and pulling up soaked flooring. He was fixing things using actual power tools. (Note: check middle son's DNA.)

I did make the mistake of going upstairs and peeking into the bedrooms. Inside each room it looked like a laundromat had exploded. Clearly, young people have decided that it is easier to get dressed every morning if you can just reach down and select from a wide smorgasbord of clothes on the floor.

And yes, there were a few cigarette butts and "empties" scattered on the porch and front lawn (and by "few" I mean several thousand). But, generally, things were in pretty good shape. All in all, I don't really mind them having the house.

Now, if they would just start paying the mortgage.

58

The Basement That Stole Christmas

December 21, 2013

Okay kids, gather round. It's time for Uncle Paul's Christmas story.

What's that? You'd rather play Xbox? You've got the new *Grand Theft Auto V*? How old are you anyway? Uh, huh. Remind me to talk to your mother later.

Okay, settle in. Pass Uncle Paul his nice glass of Christmas cheer.

This is the story of The Basement That Stole Christmas.

Once upon a time, there came to a household a terrible scourge. What's that? A scourge? It's a bad thing. Something that causes great suffering — like your math class.

Anyway, this terrible blight came upon our family. What's a blight? Oh, never mind. There came three dark forces: One was a wet and mouldy thing called Leaky Basement. He was soggy and smelly and he brought floods and pestilence.

Beside him was an old and cracked creature who cried and cried and his tears formed a river through our family's basement. He was called Weeping Tile.

And with them came the most vile of the three. He was a dark and noxious force of great mystery. He was known as Seeping Sewage of Unknown Origin.

These three descended upon our family in the days before the Christmas Season. They came with great fury and a kind of swampy pong that filled the whole house and that no air freshener could challenge. They formed a team of destruction — The Forces of Short-Term Financial Ruin.

Now, men of great learning knew that darkness and destruction could come at any time and they would prepare to do battle. No Billy, not with swords, but with a great shield, called the Emergency Fund. This is a chest filled with gold and silver equal to three months' salary. No Billy, "salary" not "celery." Listen, go get Uncle Paul another drink.

But when our hero checked for the fund it was not there, for it had been fecklessly squandered on the evils of Unlimited Data Plans, Impulse Buying, and Lousy but Expensive Casual Dining. He was filled with remorse and the home was rife with mutual blaming and frenzied threats of a Great and Terrible Austerity Budget to come.

In the meantime, soldiers of good, who looked remarkably like plumbers, came to battle Leaky Basement. They had awesome weapons — jackhammers and picks, shovels and drills — and a great tumult and clattering filled the house.

There was a mighty battle, and each time the soldiers drove out Leaky Basement, he and his odorous brethren (No Billy, Odorous Brethren is not a band, but I guess it could be) would mock them and move to a new wall.

The great battle raged for days and then weeks, and the most elusive foe was Seeping Sewage, and his scent filled the home until visitors would ask, "Are you cooking cabbage or what?"

Finally, the workers rebuilt the walls and drove back the floods and the warriors Sump Pump and Drain Flush beat the foes and even the dank smell of Seeping Sewage was smote — with the help of many vanilla-scented candles of great expense.

But our family was not out of the woods yet. No kids, brace yourselves, for what came next was the greatest terror of all: the Invoice from Hell. (Yes Billy, I think that actually is a band.) And the Invoice from Hell caused in our hero great wailing and gnashing of teeth, even with his dental appliance in place.

A dark sorrow descended on the home because the basement had Stolen Christmas.

Yea, though there would be dryness and a lack of swampy odour, alas there would be no cheer. But then, like a miracle, a shining light came out of the financial darkness.

It was Little Baby Visa!

And with Little Baby Visa came the Angel, Home Equity Line of Credit, and three semi-wise men from a Banking Land far away: Unsecured Personal Line of Credit, the much-abused Overdraft Protection, and finally Uncle Vito, who always carries a roll of hundreds that could choke a camel. But you gotta watch the "vig."

And so Little Baby Visa saved Christmas and there was much rejoicing and a fair bit of fruitcake eating.

The End.

59

My Wife, the Socks Maniac

January 18, 2014

A few days ago, I come home to find my wife in the family room, surrounded by socks.

I don't mean a few socks — you know, a half-dozen pairs that she's rolled into nice balls.

No, no. I mean a great many socks. Enough socks to cover every square inch of the room. I mean socks draped all over the couch, over chairs, on the ottoman, on the floor, and in plastic laundry hampers. There were (and I'm not kidding) 236 (147 dark, 89 white) socks in the room. I know because I counted them.

In the middle of this sock explosion sits my wife with the kind of empty look that soldiers and some bingo players get. She isn't upset so much as dazed and confused, a bit like Daisy in that scene in *The Great Gatsby* where Gatsby throws all the beautiful coloured shirts at her from the balcony, except there's no balcony in our family room and the silk shirts are actually mostly smelly gym socks. But otherwise, quite similar.

When I see this sock mess, I start to sing, "A little party never hurt nobody! So we gon' dance until we drop!" And I do what I think is a cute little dance right there in the middle of Crazy Sock World. I think this is amusing. My wife does not.

"What are you doing?" I say, intelligently.

"What does it look like I'm doing? Playing Scrabble?" she says.

She actually IS playing Scrabble on the iPad beside her, something she does quite a lot now to stop her, as she says, "from going crazy."

I decide this is probably not a good time to call the family room Crazy Sock World. I will save that for a humorous dinner conversation with guests that will result in me sleeping on the couch.

I should probably explain how this unusual sock situation transpired. Over the holidays, I may have casually mentioned that my sock drawer contained one white gym sock with a hole in it, two unmatched black socks, and a pair of red argyle socks that you only really wear at Christmas. That single pair worked for a while, but then people started avoiding me at parties. I thought it might be time to tell my wife that although I had purchased a dozen pairs of new socks in the last few months, I had none to wear.

"Fine," she said, "I'll go through the socks this week."

Having seen the baskets of socks in the basement near the dryer, I knew this was no small deal, but I kept quiet. I should be clear that in our home we have a scrupulously fair division of household duties. For example, my wife is responsible for all the laundry — washing, drying, and folding. She usually does this on Sundays.

Similarly, I am responsible on Sundays for watching NFL football. This arrangement was struck after I washed a couple of loads of laundry in which somehow every item in our household turned an interesting shade of pink. Who knew you can't put red panties in with bed sheets and towels?

Anyway, what we were staring at in the family room was 236 single socks. I know that sounds crazy, but it's true. We have searched for the missing socks in the bedrooms, the hampers, the basement — everywhere. They're gone. It's like some kind of strange mysterious phenomenon of nature, like the Higgs boson or Donald Trump's hair.

Where in God's name do the other socks go? Does someone steal them? What can you do with 236 single socks anyway? Do they dematerialize somehow, ending up in some Single Sock Dimension? Is the whole thing some kind of giant cosmic riddle, like the Big Bang Theory or why the Kardashians are famous? I don't know.

All I know is I am starting 2014 with seven matched pairs of socks and 236 single socks of varying stripes, colours, and checks. My solution is that I've decided to start wearing unmatched socks to work. If anyone asks, I'll just say, "No worries. I have other ones just like these at home."

60

It's a Be-Mine Field

February 15, 2014

If this is Saturday morning and Friday evening has come and gone, then I have survived another Valentine's Day.

As most people know, this is no easy task. Of all the fretful celebratory days that seem to multiply across the calendar each year (do we really need a day for everything from parents to pets?), I think Valentine's Day is the worst.

If, like many people, you don't have someone to celebrate with, you pass the day slightly anxious and perhaps a little forlorn. If you do have someone with whom to celebrate, you're just anxious.

First, you have to actually remember it's Valentine's Day. Yes, ten thousand pink hearts in Shoppers Drug Mart will probably remind you it's coming but you still have to remember it that day. You WILL remember though — because not remembering is right up there with forgetting your anniversary or forgetting your spouse at the mall and driving home for a nap.

No, you WILL remember and then the problem is what to do about it. After several decades of frantic, last-minute gift-buying, I'll admit I'm pretty much out of ideas. Dinner out? Usually too tired. Anyway, too expensive. Flowers? Not bad, but predictable and expensive. And often smelly — especially lilies.

Chocolates? Delicious but fattening. Candy? Not as delicious and still fattening. Just a card looks cheap. A card and jewellery looks guilty.

Frankly, I yearn for the simpler days of grade one, or perhaps it was kindergarten, before notions of romance tainted the day, when every kid — boy and girl — simply gave a Valentine's card to every single other kid. No gender worries, no exceptions. Here's a little card: Be My Valentine. Everyone! Simple, almost unconscious love that moved in all directions — lighthearted in the true sense of the word.

It's so much more complicated today. Relationships are complex and challenging. For years I thought we, my circle of close friends, lived in a kind of lucky bubble, untouched, it seemed, by marital strife. We had dinner parties and summer cottaging and raising kids and the occasional trip together and it all was good. If people drifting into middle age were no longer "madly in love," they certainly seemed, well, "solidly in love."

I know now, that was mostly just a trick of time. Wait long enough and trouble comes. As the years passed, the calls — not too many, thankfully — did come. You know, the ones that begin, "Did you hear about …?" or the more painful, "I'm just calling to let you know that …"

And what is there to say? You mumble, "I'm really sorry," and wonder what happened and why. Often it is impossible to know why — even for the people involved.

And wondering about fault or blame is even more pointless. No one really knows another couple, the things that pass between two people, sometimes not even the couple themselves. And if you need to find fault, then it's good to remember that a couple is a dynamic, a tricky dance of giving and taking and taking and giving. As my mother often wisely says, "It takes two to tango."

Who knows what keeps people together or what drives them apart? I don't, though I have come to trust a few things. I know talking is better than not talking. Though too much talking can be a problem, too. Respect is important. It's the grease in the gears of a good working relationship. And, I have come to believe that luck plays a big role.

Accidents, sickness, and tragedies of all kinds can and do come crashing in, sending us in directions and on journeys we never imagined.

Perhaps love is like gravity — hugely powerful and strangely fragile — holding two people together in an orbit while the ever-spinning universe does its best to fling them apart.

It is finally, I think, impossible to know. You muddle along the best you can in the face of it all. And as anyone who has lived long enough knows, it will be difficult. As my eighty-six-year-old mother reminds me, being positive helps.

And don't forget the flowers.

61

Dazed and Confused in the Grocery Aisle

March 1, 2014

Last Saturday I got lost.

Of course, this is not really much of a surprise to anyone who knows me. I have such a keen sense of direction that I have been known to lose my way in a shopping mall.

This is funny until the guy in the Gap wonders why you are in his store for the third time in two hours and calls security. I once tried to use the underground PATH in Toronto (a series of connected subterranean walkways) and was down there for several days. I enjoyed it — you can practically live on souvlaki! — but eventually a search and rescue team found me and took me home.

My wife and I routinely lose our way driving up north, even to cottages we have been to many times. I talk a lot, neither of us reads signs, and I usually have pretty much no idea where I'm going. "It's up the 400," my wife says.

"What exit?" I say.

"You know the one. You'll recognize it when you see it."

For sure. This strategy has led us to Muskoka — via Sudbury.

Anyway, this time I didn't get lost in a car.

I got lost in Fortinos.

Yes, that's right. Last Saturday I was standing with my shopping cart utterly bewildered in a store I've shopped in for almost twenty years.

As I was frozen there, I noticed a neighbour, Susan, go by clutching several items in her arms. We said hello. After a minute (I'm still standing there dazed and confused) I see Susan coming by again, this time the other way, juggling even more items in her arms. "I can't find pickles," she says, slightly alarmed. "Or my husband."

I realize at this point, I am not alone. I see another neighbour stumbling holding a grocery list and wearing an expression that says, "For god's sake, where are they hiding the Grey Poupon?"

I should explain that after years of practice, I am actually quite an effective grocery shopper. My battle plan each week is clear: Enter and move to produce. Chat with clerk. Head into meat. Chat with butcher. Swing around to deli. Chat with my neighbour Dave who seems to be in the salami area most of Saturday. Stand around the lobster tank for a while. (Okay, I'm odd. My parents never took us to SeaWorld.) Down middle aisles for snack bars, pop, and other almost-food products. Swing along to bread and then to dairy. Guide overflowing cart to checkout. Flip through magazines, which all seem to be about comparing Kim Kardashian's bum to Missouri. (Missouri is smaller.) Chat with checkout lady. Sample free wine. More chat. Time shopping: 52 minutes. Total time: 3.5 hours.

So I know the store. I'm lost now because after decades of being able to shop the store in a rush or half-awake or hung over, someone decided to MOVE THINGS AROUND.

And now nothing makes any sense — at least not to me. Spices are across from a rack of Vachon cakes. Canned beans are beside ethnic foods, but dried beans are in another aisle. Tuna is across from the granola bars. It's food chaos! Even stranger is what I call "The Last Chance Shelf for Unfortunate Products That No One Seems to Want." This is where you'll find boxes of hair dye beside curry pudding, green maraschino cherries, and other not-so-great food ideas. Bewildered, I ask a manager what is going on.

"We're reorganizing the store," he says.

"Yes, I noticed," I say. "But why?"

"Just for laughs, really. We move stuff around at night and then the group of us sit and watch shoppers on the video monitors upstairs. It's a riot."

Okay, I'm kidding.

What he actually told me is that they rearranged the store to make it "consistent with the layout of other Fortinos stores." Unfortunately, this is exactly why I do not shop in other locations — because when I go there, I CAN'T FIND ANYTHING.

Anyway, after a few shopping trips, I am getting used to the new layout and can now almost complete my shopping in less than a working day.

Unless I run into Dave, of course. Then all bets are off.

62

The Great Escape:
What's Wrong with My House?

March 29, 2014

We have two frogs loose in our house.

They are Korean fire belly frogs.

(I think I had "Korean fire belly" a few nights ago after some very spicy ribs, but that's another story.)

I wasn't that worried about the frogs. Sure, it's slightly unnerving to think that amphibians are running rampant through your household, but I figured, hey, they're only little frogs.

These frogs are about the size of large gummy bears, they eat live crickets, and they're pretty easy to spot with their lime green backs and bright orange and black bellies. They look like Halloween candies with eyes. (Note to self: new idea for gross holiday confection.)

I mean, sure you might get a start if one of these showed up in your bed or in your Cream of Wheat, but I figured they're small and pretty harmless.

Was I wrong?

My son, who is the keeper of the frogs, informed me that the Korean fire belly frog actually emits a toxin when surprised or angered. Since I am not totally sure what angers frogs (Do they hate the Ninja Turtles? Are they jealous of Kermit?), this information was, understandably, unsettling. Now, instead of having two tiny frogs loose in the house, perhaps desperate for food and water, we had potential frog assassins roaming around on the knife edge of amphibian rage.

Of course, this was not the first time that animals of one sort or another had broken out of their cages in our house. No, we have a long — and mostly furry — history of errant pets. In fact, our house is like *The Great Escape* of pets. We've had escaped mice, gerbils, and hamsters. We've had birds that have broken free and fluttered around the house. In fact, the only pets that have not smashed the shackles of their pet existence have been fish. No, that's not right. We even had a fish — a particularly determined goldfish — who did indeed escape the bowl by launching himself (or herself, it's so hard to tell — even for other goldfish) out of the water, out of the bowl, and right onto the dining room table. There it became clear that goldfish, while good at the initial elements of escape, are clearly not so good about follow-up issues — like a good disguise and BREATHING.

Now that I think about it, this problem with household pets stretches all the way back to my own childhood. My father, who hated cats and loved dogs — as long as they were someone ELSE'S dogs — had very strict ideas around pets. Birds, particularly canaries, were okay, and so were fish. Anything that barked, shed, and the other "s-word" in the house was out. Anything that whistled or gurgled and did not need to be walked was fine — and that included relatives.

Anyway, back to the Korean fire belly. (I'm feeling much better now, thank you, but believe me it wasn't pretty.) And back to the frogs. My son James, who is conscientious about his animals, was sad they had escaped, knowing their fate was sealed. It would be an understatement to say our basement is "not conducive to supporting life of any kind." In fact, it's like Jupiter, only messier.

My wife was even more concerned, worried the frogs would show up at an inopportune time — say, during a dinner party.

Wife: "Yes, the first course is a nice kale salad, with cranberries and Asiago cheese."

Guest: (looking at plate) "Is this frog decorative? Or did I miss some kind of Chinese holiday?"

Wife: "Here, let me get that. The frogs are for another course."

She has a right to be worried. At various times, our house has had trouble with what we will politely call "unwanted guests" and I don't mean my cousin Carmine. I am not allowed to ever speak about this, but let's just say that what once got into our house rhymes with "hat," but you wouldn't want one on your head.

Anyway, one of the frogs showed up this week in James's room, in remarkably good health.

"How did it survive?" I asked.

"Oh, it probably fed on all the crickets that are loose in the house," he said.

Perfect.

63

Who Knew They Were Listening?

April 26, 2014

Like many people, I am worried about identity theft.

I have been reading about the latest computer security problem, Heartbleed, and I can tell you authoritatively that I have no idea what anyone is talking about. But I'm pretty sure that if I understood even half of what it is, I'd be even more worried. Luckily, I can't get past lines like "The code was part of a 2011 update to Open SSL designed for encryption of transferred data …," so it doesn't really matter.

I did understand that my online information may be "vulnerable to hackers," particularly because of the extremely sophisticated system I use for passwords. In a moment of what I like to think of as sheer genius but which my wife calls "almost crazy-level laziness," I decided to use reverse psychology on my password and make it so dumb and easy that no one in their right mind would believe a grown man would use it. Unfortunately, this turned out to be a theory used by many other people, and using the word *password* for your password is not all that clever. Who knew?

In any case, I'm not sure I care. If legions of brilliant Chinese hackers want to break through my security and take over my online banking, let them! What they'll get is access to a line of credit that could easily buy a family of four a modest lunch (no apps or drinks), and a mountain of debt that could destabilize Beijing. No, it's not cyberhackers I'm worried about. It's the threat closer to home.

I say this because of troubling recent incidents of what I think could be either A. very complex identify theft or B. my own sheer stupidity. (Again, my wife is leaning toward B.)

Recently, I went to my local branch of the public library to take out some books. I have told my children about this amazing place filled with books and magazines and DVDs, and they say, "Yes Dad, we know. It's called Chapters. Stop blathering on and give us your credit card" or words to that effect. Anyway, I took a couple of books up to the front desk, handed over my card, and noticed that the pleasant woman behind the counter gave me an odd look and uttered the words you never want to hear at the library.

"Excuse me, Mr. Benduti, but you seem to have some overdue fines."

"No, I don't think so," I said, confidence draining out of me as I pictured the stack of unread books by my bedside.

"Actually it's quite a list here," she said. "And they're very overdue."

"Really?" I said. "How overdue?"

"Well, after a while we stop counting and just charge you the maximum fine. You owe ... let me see ... $45.50."

"What! You've got to be kidding," I say.

"Sir, please step away from the counter and stop yelling."

"Okay, sorry," I say. "What are the books?"

"Two on shopping, one about Paris fashions, and the last two books in The Hunger Games series," she says. "You also have several DVDs out. *The Lizzie McGuire Movie* with Hilary Duff and *The Sweetest Thing* with Christina Applegate," she says, raising an eyebrow. "Did you enjoy those?"

"There must be some mistake," I say, a bit louder than I had hoped. A small crowd is gathering. "I don't even like Hilary Duff. Well, maybe some of her early work, but just the same, I did not take out these ..."

And then it hits me. My daughter. Clearly, she took my advice. And my library card.

"Would you like cash or can I use my credit card?" I say, quietly.

"Based on your record, I'd say cash," she says, politely. "And please return those books as soon as possible."

I drive home, and sure enough, in well under two hours I find the books and DVDs in my daughter's room on the floor under about three tons of clothes. I'm about to drive directly back to the library when I stop, flip open the case, and pop in *The Lizzie McGuire Movie*. Hell, I might as well watch it.

I bought it — about four times.

64

My Mother:
She Was Not Special ... But She Was

May 10, 2014

Her breathing had changed, so my sisters asked the nurse to come in. It was shallow now and slower. We knew the sound. We remembered it from my dad. The nurse checked her pulse. My mother was resting nicely, calmed by the painkillers coursing through her body, eyes closed, mouth slightly ajar. Her small chest rose and fell, but slower, with longer pauses between. Janice, our gentle, caring nurse turned to us. "It won't be long now."

It is Sunday, May 4, a little past three in the afternoon. The late-day sun is streaming through the windows of her room. It is one week before Mother's Day.

My mother was not a special person.

She did not build a business or write a great book. She did not hold public office or win awards. She was born October 23, 1927, at home, in a small bungalow at the corner of MacNab Street North and Strachan Street. Except for three years when we moved to Ottawa for my dad's job, she lived her entire life in Hamilton. She got married and raised kids. She cooked our meals and sewed our clothes. She kept house, though not that well, to be honest. On May 4, at 4:42 p.m. on a bright spring Sunday afternoon, she died. She was eighty-six.

I realized something in the past weeks and days, though I think I had always known it. I thought about it when I sat with her at the hospital and

I talked about it with my brothers and sisters. My mother was not special and she was. And if that sounds like a contradiction, it is.

The end started a few months ago, although of course, we did not know that then. She had a minor heart attack in November and seemed to recover, though not fully. Then she had another in February and that one, much more serious, landed her back in the hospital.

At first, it seemed as if this would go the same way it had when she broke her hip two years ago. Operation, rehab, and out. Back to her place, to her friends at St. Elizabeth Village, back to her independent life.

I think she believed that, too, and although her heart had suffered considerable damage, she put on a good show and was deemed a candidate for rehabilitation.

So, we found ourselves back at Juravinski Hospital, but little else was the same. For the first few weeks, Mom tried her best to follow instructions, to get up each day, to get behind her walker, to build herself back up. She knew the milestones she had to hit to get out and she tried. Her goal was to go home and she told everyone that's where she was going. But her energy, her signature boundless energy, was low. She tired easily. Taking her walker down the hall would tap her out for the day. Some days, even a few steps left her winded, panting by her bedside.

"I don't understand," she said, between wheezes.

"It's okay, Mom. You're just tired. Tomorrow will be better."

But tomorrow was not better and it dawned on her that this would not be a repeat performance of her recovery from hip surgery; that something had changed. One day she said, "I know I can't go home." It was a hard truth, but she accepted it with grace and, as always, put on a brave face. We told her we would find a good place for her and she said okay, but it was not okay.

We watched her go through a kind of mini mourning cycle. Denial, which had made the rehab attempt possible, was done. Then, briefly, there was anger. Not at us or the doctor or even the lovely nurses who helped her each day, but at herself.

"What's wrong with me?" she asked, one day, sitting on her bed, exhausted. "I never thought I would be like this."

But she was, and the realization of it — admitting it — broke something in her. A deep fatigue seemed to wash over her.

She was so thoroughly exhausted, she could not find words, could not finish a sentence without her eyes fluttering shut. When the nurses asked if she would like to get up to walk, she would shake her head no and gently say, "Not today."

"Maybe tomorrow?"

"Yes, maybe tomorrow."

My mother, born Mary Rita Carpani, loved tomorrows. But she loved todays even better. She had an unfettered optimism, an untainted enthusiasm, and a rare capacity to embrace life in all its complexity with real humility and with a sense of gratitude. She was happy. Not in some mindless silly way, but deeply happy, blessed, she would say, by all the riches that life offered.

Not riches in the usual sense. She cared little for money. In fact, not at all. She grew up without it, a child of the Great Depression. Her family lived a block from the Hamilton Bay and, like many families, survived for several years on "relief." At Christmas, she would tell us, she and her five siblings were thrilled if they found in their stockings some walnuts and a fresh orange. "Treasures," she said. They had good food and what they had they shared. Always a sandwich and a cup of coffee for the men who walked up from the rail lines that ran behind their house, looking for a meal. That generosity never waned, and later, when she felt blessed to have some money in savings, she gave it away. Constantly. To her children and her grandchildren, for school or books or birthdays or for no reason at all.

What can I tell you about her? Graduated from Westdale Secondary. Worked as a seamstress downtown until she married. Sewed her own clothes. Never once smoked a cigarette. Walked every day. Had five children: Joe, Paul, Rosanne, Paula, and Robert. Liked a glass of wine, usually rosé. Sometimes, for fun, a shot of Baileys.

She was Catholic and had faith, but pushed it on no one. She loved to dance — waltz, foxtrot, tarantella, tango. She had a nice voice and knew the words to dozens and dozens of songs. Standards. She liked Romano better than Parmigiano. She had a high school diploma. She read every book in the syllabus of my honours degree in English literature.

She knew the dialect of Le Marche, but taught herself to speak proper Italian. She was maybe five-foot-three, shorter as she aged. She was almost twenty-six when she married, old for the time. She liked rice pudding.

My eldest sister, Rosanne, said that in all the years she raised us, she never, never once, said an unkind thing to her. Or any of us.

She enjoyed each day and looked forward to each tomorrow.

But tomorrow was the same. Worse. Soon, even the simple act of sitting up or eating a few teaspoons of her breakfast tapped what little energy she had left. We would spoon-feed her, encourage her to eat a bit a more, to take a few sips of milk.

One day, on Tuesday, I came in to find her dressed, slumped in her wheelchair asleep, her head awkwardly drooped forward. Her arms, stick thin, were mottled with wine-coloured bruises from the blood tests and the IV lines.

I woke my mother and she said hello and I asked her if she wanted to go back to bed. It was mid-morning.

"Yes," she said.

The nurse and I gently raised her from her wheelchair and her tiny body sagged against us, limp in our arms. I swung her legs into bed and then leaned over her to smooth her blanket. When I did, she whispered to me, "I can't do this anymore."

"You don't have to, Mom," I said. "You don't have to."

That day, I told my siblings what she had already figured out and what we in some ways had known, but could not admit.

My sisters, Rosanne and Paula, and I sat down with the doctor, who confirmed what in our hearts we already knew. My mother was not rehabbing. She was not getting better. She would never get better. There was no procedure to fix her, no medicine to make her well.

They took out the IV line that was causing her so much discomfort. They moved her to a private room with two big windows that caught the spring sunshine.

My mother had something, an undefinable quality, that was evident to anyone who met her. People liked her. Immediately. She made them smile. One day a couple of months back, I was at St. Elizabeth Village to give a talk at the monthly "ladies lunch." On my way into the village centre, a small bus pulled up and abruptly stopped. A man jumped out and walked toward me.

"Are you Paul Benedetti?" he asked.

"Yes," I said.

"I'm Dave. Dave the bus driver."

"Yes Dave, my mom talks about you all the time," I said.

"How is she?" he asked.

I explained how she was not recovering as we had hoped. I was careful, but honest.

"I take her all around," he said. "To Fortinos and shopping at the mall."

"I know," I said. "Thank you so much."

He paused and stood for a moment in front of me.

"I love your mother," he said.

"I know," I said. "We all do."

These things happened so often, we all grew used to it, though never quite. "Your mother is Mary?" people would ask. "She's amazing."

On Wednesday, we all sat with her. She rested. And then on Thursday, as sometimes happens, she rallied. Freed from the struggle of trying so hard, she was able to pool her energy, whatever reserves she had left, for one last go.

I came in that afternoon to find my mother sitting up in bed, her eyes bright, smiling and talking to my sisters.

"She's been like this for a while," my sister Rosanne said, smiling. "She's back."

That day she smiled and talked in full sentences and joked, and, as the grandchildren came in, she greeted each by name and soon the room was full, overflowing. An orderly brought more chairs and, just like that, a party broke out in Room Seven, Floor Two of M Wing.

And then, after a couple of wonderful hours, her eyes fluttered and she grew tired and the grandkids and kids kissed her soft, warm face and said their goodbyes to grandma and we settled her into bed and she fell asleep, smiling.

"That was it," I said to my siblings. "That was all she had."

We knew what was next. We had all been here before, six years before, with our father. And my mother knew best of all.

On Friday, at her request, we called the priest and she received the Sacrament of the Sick. The doctor had explained the plan, the medications for pain. The nurses would make sure she was comfortable.

"I can't give you a timeline," the doctor said. "Could be days, for some people it's weeks."

But we knew it would not be weeks. Our mother was spent. The dynamo that had fuelled her tiny body for so long had finally run out. We used to joke that she was like the Energizer Battery Bunny, always moving, always talking, a whirlwind of energy and enthusiasm. But now that battery had run down and she was still.

On Friday, she tried to rest, but she grew agitated, moaning, going in and out. She asked, "Where is my husband?" She prayed, usually the Hail Mary, her favourite. She made us take twenty dollars for lunch. "If you give money away," she said, "the Lord gives you more."

She was uncomfortable, unable to settle. My sisters held her hands and soothed her. I leaned over her.

"When will this be over?" she asked.

"Soon," I said. "Soon."

She closed her eyes.

Saturday was hard, and as her body began to shut down she grew more restless and agitated, in clear discomfort. "Are you in pain, Mom," my sister Paula asked her.

"I don't want to be a bother," she said. "I'm like a baby."

My two sisters lovingly tended to her. The doctor upped her meds and the nurses helped with the pain, and her faith helped with the rest. She would pray quietly and every now and then say, "Thy will be done."

She knew the journey she was on and she did not complain and she was not afraid.

And when Sunday came, I knew it would be our last day with her and we gathered in her room and each of us said what we had to say, though there was little need because we had told her many times before as she had so often told us.

The afternoon sun poured through the windows, and on May 4, at 4:42 p.m. the final breath of life went out of her and she was still.

After a while, we gathered in the hall outside her room and Janice, the small, gentle nurse with sad eyes who had cared for her through the weekend, walked toward us and stopped.

"I am sorry for your loss," she said, her voice shaking a little. "I wanted to tell you that it has been an honour to be with your family. Your mother was a beautiful person and she was surrounded by love."

And my sister Rosanne said, "That's because she loved so much."

My mother was not a special person and she was. She had in her quiet, modest way figured it out. She had solved life's puzzle, the problem we wrestle with each day. How do I live a good life? How can I be happy? She had done that, naturally and with grace and it was all there, right there to see for anyone who took a moment to look.

I was looking now, again, and realized something I had somehow known for a long time, but had not quite seen.

We were in the hall, a few hours before my mother died and Rosanne had just leaned in close to my mom's smooth, unlined face to kiss her and tell her, again, how much she loved her, how much we all loved her.

"I told her she was the best mother anyone could have," she said, the tears streaming down her face.

And I told her the thing I had finally come to understand. That my mother, my small, beautiful, humble mother, was the best person I had ever known.

65

Seawalls, Coffee Shops, and Used Books

May 24, 2014

Every few years my wife's sisters in Hamilton decide it's time to share my charms with her three sisters in Vancouver.

I point out to them that travelling three thousand kilometres and taking a week off is no small deal, but they are extremely encouraging, often pooling their own resources for my ticket and calling my employer to arrange my vacation. They're amazing.

Anyway, that's how we found ourselves in Vancouver recently walking along the city's famous seawall. When you're in the city, you can immediately spot the locals; they're the ones staring at their cellphones and running into poles. The rest of us are gawking at the mountains and running into poles.

There are many things you notice about the city almost as soon as you arrive.

As we walked around I kept thinking, what am I missing here that we have at home? And then it hit me: garbage! Vancouver is extremely clean. I'm not sure how they do it. Maybe, if you drop your espresso cup, city workers dressed in Lululemon outfits skip by and pick it up, I don't know. But it's spotless.

You also notice there are a lot of coffee shops. I don't mean the usual ridiculous number of Tim Hortons all over our city. I mean A LOT of coffee shops. When you're in a coffee shop in Vancouver, you can look out the window and see ANOTHER COFFEE SHOP. At some intersections (I'm not kidding) there are coffee shops on every corner. I think recently someone opened a coffee shop INSIDE a coffee shop.

Because of all the coffee they drink, a lot of people in Vancouver are running. They run along the seawall, they run with their dogs (who also may be drinking coffee). I think they're running mostly to find a bathroom. You try drinking a triple espresso latte and going for a jog.

One day, my wife and I took the ferry to Victoria. I recommend this trip very highly. Not only do you get the thrill of driving a car onto a boat, but the scenery on the way over is absolutely spectacular.

Victoria itself is also beautiful. In some ways it's a lot like Vancouver. There are many people there also wearing Lululemon, but because it's a retirement community, the people are not running, they're walking. You do notice a lot of nicely dressed people with grey hair. One cab driver told us the city had more than one thousand drivers over the age of ninety. I kept that in mind when I crossed a street.

The city is full of old-world charm, and one of the places I had to visit was Munro's Books in Victoria's Old Town. The store, started by Jim Munro and his then wife, Alice (yes, the Nobel Prize–winning Alice), now resides in a stately bank building filled with enough books to shake a stick at, if that is your idea of a good time. There are no dishes or candles or picture frames in sight. Just books. I was in there trying to find an old book by Elmore ("Dutch") Leonard, one of his early westerns called *Valdez Is Coming*. They had lots of Leonard's books but not that one. The young lady who helped me said, "Have you tried Russell Books? It's just down the street."

So, I walked two blocks and found the most amazing used book store I have ever seen. Shelves and shelves of books — thousands of them, row upon row. A young woman who seemed to know where every book in the store was walked me straight to the Leonard shelves. They had dozens and dozens of back titles, but not *Valdez Is Coming*. She kindly offered to order it in for me, but I told her I was just visiting.

"From where?" she said.

"Hamilton. It's near Toronto," I said.

"I know. My dad was from Hamilton."

We had a nice chat. I asked her how her family ended up way out here. Turned out her father came west to go to school.

"He never went back?" I said.

"He met a girl. My mother," she smiled.

I bought a book anyway. I could have bought a hundred.

I know I can find the book online or download it, but you can't smell books online.

And nobody smiles at you when you check out.

66

Anchors Away

July 19, 2014

July is a time when many Canadians pack their cars, put the dogs in the back seat, kennel the kids, and head off to the cottage. (There's something wrong with that sentence, but I can't quite figure it out. Oh, yes, you're supposed to put dogs in a travel crate. Sorry.)

The most important thing about your summer vacation is not that you are going to a nice cottage, but only that you are going to someone ELSE'S cottage. What many people call their Summer Vacation, I like to call Summer Freeloading.

This is where you casually ask friends and relatives what they are doing for the summer. Once you find out, you fake surprise that you are "off at exactly the same time!" and could easily "drop in" for a visit. Then you phone work and book those weeks off.

In fact, I just returned from almost two weeks of Summer Freeloading that I think went quite well, all things considered, and by "all things considered," I mean several fairly large problems that involved the police and a rather sizeable insurance claim. But no matter. The key is that you have a lovely holiday in Canada's north — free of charge!

Our vacation was at my brother-in-law John's cottage on the St. Lawrence River in the Thousand Islands. The "cottage" is actually a century-old farmhouse complete with red barn and a bucolic pasture — whatever that is.

As you might imagine, a one-hundred-plus-year-old farmhouse needs a lot of upkeep and repair. I say "imagine" because that's what I did, preferring to leave the actual work to John, who seemed to be fixing something or other from morning to night. I could see him working hard from my chair on the porch, and every now and then I would pass him as I went to get a fresh beer.

Me: Wow, I didn't know you could actually get your whole head inside a toilet.

John: Yeah, well someone clogged the line with hair gel, dental floss, and about forty pounds of toilet paper this morning.

Me: Well, I have no idea (quickly putting a baseball cap over my glistening hair). Good luck with that.

The key thing to remember when you are cottage freeloading is to avoid drawing attention to yourself. I have known people who, using this technique, have stayed at a cottage the entire summer, eventually being called "Uncle Freddy" by the kids and joining the local Rotary Club. Unfortunately, this did not work for me.

On day one, I offered to make coffee in the morning. I measured out the coffee, filled the percolator with water, and plugged it into the stove's outlet. I also grabbed a frying pan and turned on a burner to start the eggs. After a few minutes, someone said, "I think I smell plastic burning." (I wish I were making this up.) To shorten this story, I'm providing the following equation:

cold frying pan + wrong burner + smoke = melted percolator.

To redeem myself, I decided to go fishing and try to catch that evening's dinner. (I also wish I were making this up.) I took my brother-in-law's boat to a good spot in a nearby channel. I carefully tied off the anchor line on a boat cleat and tossed the anchor over. In hindsight, it might have been a good idea to check the knot on the other end of the line. Because essentially what I did was expertly heave a perfectly good anchor into the depths of the St. Lawrence River, never to be seen again.

This story can be summarized as follows: lack of knot + I'm an idiot = $59.99 for new anchor.

As you might imagine, any decent, thoughtful person would offer to repay my hosts and replace everything that was lost or destroyed. I blamed everything on the kids. But my wife forced me to go to town, where I bought a new coffee maker, a new anchor, four toilet plungers, a week's worth of groceries, and several cases of good wine. This basically took the "free" out of my Summer Freeloading. The upside is, John invited me back next year.

As long as I bring a thousand dollars with me and stay in my room.

#youknowyouareoldwhen

August 2, 2014

Summer is an excellent time to sit back, relax, and reflect on the fact that you don't know anything anymore.

This condition is pretty common if you are over fifty — along with not knowing where your car keys are, being fundamentally incapable of understanding which of the three remotes you have actually turns on your TV, and always asking the same question no matter what building you walk into: "Where is the washroom?"

Other signs of being pretty much totally out of it are:

Getting in your car and realizing you've been playing the same Doobie Brothers CD for the past fourteen years (and you still have absolutely no idea what Michael McDonald is saying in "What a Fool Believes").

Trying to work the ticket kiosk at the movies, giving up, and just getting in the live-cashier line with the other seniors. Recognizing too late, like one of my good friends' mom, that LOL is not an acronym for "Lots of Love," as in: "Sorry to hear about the untimely passing of your husband. LOL."

All of these are markers that you're just not keeping up.

This weekend I was perplexed when my niece Emma kept going around saying, "Linda, honey, just listen …" and everyone would burst into gales of laughter, whatever those are. I, on the other hand, had no idea what she was talking about. Turns out she was mimicking the latest Internet meme. If you don't know what the previous sentence even means, it's time to loosen your Sansabelt slacks, pour a nice cup of Ovaltine, and concentrate. This is going to require some heavy lifting.

A meme (Remember, meme rhymes with gene. If you don't pronounce meme like them you will be even more out of it.) is a funny video or saying that spreads across the Internet. In some cases, like a bad cold.

This latest one is a short video of a toddler who is arguing with his mom, whom he calls "Linda." If that doesn't sound totally hilarious, it's because, like all of these things, you have to see it to "get" it. Once you watch it, the first thing you will think is: "Oh, that's so cute!" or more likely, "What the hell are people doing at work all day if they have time for this stuff?"

In any case, not knowing the latest hot meme is like not knowing why people keep adding "-mageddon" to everything, as in snowmageddon for some flurries or Fordmageddon for the Toronto mayoralty race (okay, that one fits). Even worse is not understanding why young guys with extremely tight pants and oddly shaggy beards keep putting the pound symbol — # — and the word for it — *hashtag* — in front of everything they say. Like this:

"How was work today?"

"Work? Are you kidding? #worksucks, #workingfortheman, #badjobs."

"Really? What's the problem?"

"Oh man. #managerswehate, #devilwearsprada, #toxicboss ..."

I could explain how all of this comes out of the "Twitterverse," but then I'd have to explain that word and "Twitter" and "tweets" and "trending topics" and "hashtags" and then we'd be back where we started.

After a while, you get the impression that somehow without you knowing it, you've been transported to another country where you don't speak the language.

Everywhere you go people are talking about "sexting" and "twerking" and "chirping" and saying stuff that doesn't even sound like words such as "YOLO" and "WOS."

But even worse than not understanding what people are saying is not really getting what people are doing. Say you go out to dinner with someone. The first thing they do is whip out their cellphone and take a picture of themselves in the restaurant and post it to Facebook or Twitter.

This is called a "selfie" and people are taking them all day, presumably because they don't really exist until their picture is online.

Then they take a picture of the food they are going to eat before they eat it and post it to Instagram so other people can see the dinner they are NOT going to eat. Then they might microblog about it at Tumblr. And if that sentence didn't make much sense to you, don't worry.

Take it from me — it's Slangmageddon out there, and anyway, we're all #toofarbehind.

68

Letting Go, One Child at a Time

August 30, 2014

If you happened to be strolling down Rue Sainte Catherine in Montreal last weekend, you may have noticed a dashing, middle-aged man, greying at the temples, nattily dressed in slim jeans and caramel-coloured brogues, and sporting a sky-blue sweater jauntily tied around his neck.

That wasn't me.

I noticed him, too, though. Boy, those French guys really know how to dress.

No, I was tottering through the fashion district, a sullen, bedraggled shell of a man, carrying thirty-seven shopping bags and an empty wallet. In front of me, occasionally turning to tell me to "keep up" were my wife and daughter, busily looking for the next store to enter and pillage with my credit card. How was I, a near-grown man, reduced to a shopping sherpa? Easy. We had driven to Montreal to take our daughter, Ella, to university. Why we were shopping for anything was a mystery to me, though, since we had packed our aging SUV with several tonnes of boxes, suitcases, and an inordinate number of clothing bags and shoes.

"I don't understand why you need seventeen pairs of shoes to go to school. When I went to school, my brother and I shared a pair of shoes. He got Monday and Wednesday. I got Tuesday and Thursday. On Friday, we each wore one shoe," I said, loading yet another rack of high heels and rubber boots into the car.

"Whatever, Dad. Don't squish my wellies."

We had packed up children before — sending our son Matthew off to Europe and our son James into the basement. We've seen little of either of them since, though I can occasionally hear James downstairs. But sending a girl off was entirely different. For one thing, we had just spent more than two hours in Montreal looking for a "duvet cover." Neither of my boys even knows what a duvet is and so would be unlikely to hunt for its cover. Essentially, it's a large fabric bag that you push a blanket into. Why you do this is beyond me, but apparently many women feel it is crucial to a good night's sleep. Also, it's very expensive because of the cost of translating the word *blanket* into French.

Anyway, after fourteen hours of shopping and two calls to the bank to extend our line of credit, we went back to the hotel. The next morning we drove across town to Ella's dorm. There, we were greeted by balloons, blasting pop music, and a bevy of blue-shirted, strapping, male McGill students ready to help you unload your car while they chatted up your daughter.

The rest of the process was a bit of a blur as we joined the throng of hundreds of students and parents shlepping suitcases, boxes, bags, and bookshelves up the elevators for the next few hours.

I have to admit the excitement was infectious, and at one point I suggested I buy a McGill hoodie and extend my stay through Frosh Week to help Ella acclimatize to her new surroundings while I practised my keg stands and funnel shots. Oddly, my wife kiboshed the idea.

Anyway, we settled Ella into her room and then went for lunch. After the noise and bustle of the morning, we now found ourselves quiet. We walked back to the dorm.

Up in her room, we both started to fuss with things and our daughter told us to stop. "I can do all that later," she said. "You guys should get going. It's a long drive."

Crying quietly, my wife hugged our daughter. And then I did. "Work hard. Have fun. Be safe," I said as I held her tight. "I love you."

"Okay, go," she said, her eyes filling with tears.

And so we did, leaving our daughter, our last child — our "baby" — to start the adventure of her own life.

And in the car the heady mix of excitement and happiness that had buoyed us up through the weekend evaporated and we sat in a kind of stunned silence. You do not own your children, I thought. Rather, you have the privilege of raising them, and somehow those years had shot by and here we were now, driving in the bright sunshine, speechless, hot tears streaming down our faces.

69

Schnapps and Skinny Suits

November 22, 2014

I knew I was in trouble when the kid looked over and said, "You up for a shot?"

"Of what?" I asked as the bartender started filling not-so-little plastic glasses.

"Peach schnapps and vodka," which immediately translated in my head to "hangover and really bad headache."

I did the shot. What can you do when a bunch of guys half your age challenge you to drink? (Well, a mature person could do a lot of things, but we're talking me here.)

But I knew I was in trouble long before the shooter bar incident.

I was at our good friends Ron and Heather's daughter's wedding. Lauren married a strapping firefighter named Justin and I was standing around trying to drink with him and his buddies. This is a bad idea for a number of reasons. One, they are all about forty years younger than I, with matching youthful livers. And two, they are in tremendous shape, with large firefighter muscles and the constitutions of plow horses. (In fact, several of them have weekend jobs as plow horses).

But I have to admit this was only one of the problems I had with the reality of this wedding.

First, when your friends' kids start getting married, it is a powerful personal and philosophical signal. And the signal says: you are OLD.

It felt like Ron and I and all the other good friends at the wedding were, only a few years ago, doing our own shooters and throwing up later. (Okay, mostly I threw up, but it's a stomach condition and not my fault). But this day was living proof that about four decades had passed without anyone noticing. These beautiful milestone events — along with having the girl at McDonald's ask if you want the "senior discount" and your first colonoscopy — help us all mark the passage of time.

If that's not enough for you, I noted several other key signs that I am old and essentially "out of it."

Skinny Suits: All the men were wearing suits that looked like they'd been left in the dryer too long. I actually like the look of these suits with their narrow pants and their fitted jackets. I like them on other people. That's because young people have skinny bodies to go into their skinny suits, whereas these suits would make me look like a standing human sausage. Good for a day job out in front of Denninger's, but bad for a wedding.

Dancing: Aging white guys have a deservedly bad reputation when it comes to dancing. We're either listlessly shuffling back and forth almost on the beat, or we're engaged in a booze-fuelled, fit-like rendition of the Funky Chicken that's scaring the bejesus out of our wives and coming dangerously close to injuring other dancers. It's not pretty. Especially compared to the young people who are working the floor like they're at a rave. Thankfully, no one tried to do the splits — and by no one, I mean me. The last time involved ripped pants, three hours in the ER, and no heavy lifting for a month.

Jokes and References You Don't Get: At this wedding, to reduce the annoying habit of glass tinkling, the DJ made tables identify theme songs from popular TV shows before the bride and groom would kiss. This was excellent except no one at our table recognized any of the songs EVEN AFTER the show title was announced. I kept yelling out, "What about *Gilligan's Island*?" while my wife punched my leg under the table. It reminded me of Sunday dinner at home.

Technology That None of Us Understands: Just after dinner, the DJ directed the guests to "the screen on the far wall," and what followed was a movie of the wedding, including video of the beautiful bride and groom, still photos, and a full soundtrack. No one knew how this was accomplished, though one friend suggested a "time machine" had been used. He had also been drinking schnapps shooters.

By the end of the night, I felt pretty old. To compensate, when I got home, I put on some James Brown and tried to do the splits.

My wife found me on the floor in the morning.

70

Next Time, It's the Full Mullet

December 6, 2014

Recently my wife interrupted me while I was pretending to do some work on my computer and asked, "How do you like my hair?"

Apparently, she had been to the hairdresser — again. I looked up and noted that her hair looked pretty good — glossy and neatly trimmed. "Nice," I said. "But I thought you just went to the hairdresser."

"Ugh, whatever," she said.

This is a touchy subject because I once actually looked at our Visa statement (Whoa! I won't do that again. I was in bed for a week!) and noted that my wife spends about fourteen thousand dollars more a year on her hair than I do. When I gently pointed this out to her one evening, she began to explain and then thought better of it and just hit me over the head with a cheeseboard that happened to be on the table.

I learned a great lesson that night: buy a smaller and lighter cheeseboard. And also, I realized that most guys really don't think about their hair that much — unless you're a game show host or Stephen Harper, who has to make sure he gets his hair rust-proofed once a year.

For example, most guys get their hair cut about every four or five weeks, usually if someone reminds them. How do you know it's time to get a haircut? A good sign is when your head hair and back hair form an uninterrupted "fur carpet" on your neck. This is a common look among older men and not a good one — unless you're a badger.

Most guys I know go to a barber, the same barber they've been going to for years. And they get pretty much the same haircut they've had since their twenties. Why their twenties? Because, if you've stuck with the haircut you had in your teens, you now resemble an aging male Charlie's Angel. Not a good look, even if you're a badger.

Personally, I don't go to a barber. I like barbers, but if I go to a barber shop there is a high probability that at some point I will have to answer a question like, "Do you think Brady can take the Patriots to the Super Bowl? And what about Peyton Manning?"

I got flustered by this once and said, "I think Manning did a good job as head of the Reform Party, but he's a bit old for the NFL." I was asked to leave the barber shop.

So, I prefer to go to a "hair stylist." You may ask, what is the difference between a barber and a stylist? The answer is: about twenty dollars and the liberal use of hair gel.

My hair stylist is Joe, and he's been cutting my hair for almost thirty years. I like Joe because he treats every haircut like it's the first.

I sit down and he says, "Okay, what are we going to do today?" He asks this with real sincerity, even though my cut hasn't changed appreciably for a couple of decades. Just once I'd like to say, "Well Joe, I've decided to shake things up a bit at work, so how about a full mullet? And let's dye it purple."

But I don't. I always say, "How about we clean up the sides and not too much off the top."

And he says cheerfully, "Good idea!"

It's really the only idea, because like most men, I have hair on the sides and not much on the top. So what other direction would I give? If I said, let's trim up the top and leave the sides, I'd look like Bozo the Clown, thus aligning my haircut with the general impression people have of me.

So Joe starts cutting and we start talking — about our kids, the city, music — and the more we talk, the more Joe cuts. Once, we got into a pretty involved discussion about local politics and I came out looking like a marine cadet. Now, I'm more careful.

I talk a bit less, he cuts a bit less (hell, there's less to cut) and nobody mentions Tony Romo, though I think it's a pretty good restaurant.

71

"The Twelve Ways of Christmas"

December 20, 2014

Everything, it seems, comes in twelves at Christmas time.

The Twelve Days of Christmas, the twelve people you are forced to invite for dinner, the twelve pounds you put on between now and New Year's Day, and the same twelve Christmas CDs you play over and over until finally someone screams, "Make it stop! Make it stop!" and falls on the floor thrashing around. (Okay, that last one is me and it usually happens right after the 147th hearing of Burl Ives's "Holly Jolly Christmas.")

Let's face it, the Christmas season is a mix of good and, well, not-so-good things. So, along with your to-do list, your gift list, and your Christmas dinner grocery list, here's my list: Twelve (Good and Bad) Things About Christmas.

1. Driving to the mall and circling around the lot for about twenty minutes trying to find an open spot and then finding one and getting into an altercation with the guy who drives up at the last second and steals the spot and then driving around some more and then banging on the dashboard hysterically and driving home.
2. Eggnog. Super fattening. And delicious.
3. The dreaded office Christmas party. Being forced to chat with Manny the office weasel who also eats with his mouth open?

Listening to Eleanor complain, only now she's wearing an elf hat? Having drinks with your manager, who just announced that down-sizing starts in January? I'd rather have the flu.

4. Receiving the few — now rare — real Christmas cards in the mail. Old-fashioned cards with a winter scene on the front and a handwritten message inside. They're like missives from the past, vestiges of a time before email and texting, when the slow flow of handwriting made people pause and think about what they wanted to say. I especially like the card I get from my pal Wayne, who, each year, turns a photograph he's taken into a handmade card and then gets his wife, who has better penmanship, to scribe a lovely note. It sits on our mantel, a lonely reminder of Christmas before the Internet.

5. The Italian Christmas Eve Feast of the Seven Fishes. My wife says it makes the house smell for seven days, but who cares?

6. The dreaded "Christmas Family Update Letter." Okay, your daughter got into Harvard, you were promoted to vice-president, your golf holiday in Jamaica was perfect, and your dog just got inducted into Mensa. It just wouldn't be Christmas without hearing about your money, your gifted kids, and your perfect life. I'd love to write back, but I've got to go to the food bank, get my car out of repo — again — and, oh yeah, my motorhome is on fire.

7. Waking up Christmas morning and having panettone with coffee and Baileys. Super fattening. And delicious.

8. Buying a twenty-dollar environmentally friendly Christmas tree at Ikea and getting a twenty-dollar coupon back! Made getting in and out of the parking lot worth it.

9. Finding a hundred-dollar gift card in the last year's wrapping-paper box that expired two months ago.

10. Mashed rutabaga. Mashed parsnips. Mashed turnip. Not even babies will eat it.

11. Leaving a bottle of wine for the mailman because he makes it to your door every day, rain or sleet or snow, and he's always smiling.

12. Driving to Niagara Falls with my brothers to attend the Christmas party for my developmentally delayed cousin Julia Mary. It was

held in an old fire hall and the staff of their group home made a full Christmas dinner, including turkey, stuffing, and all the trimmings. Julia, who is now in her late forties, was there with her three roommates as well as a handful of other residents and their families. We had non-alcoholic punch, ate our dinner, sang Christmas carols (badly, and nobody cared) and waited for Santa to arrive. The residents, no matter what their ages, retain a childlike excitement about Christmas and they erupted in squeals and cheers when Santa arrived. They got their presents, we danced around the room in a conga line, and the "kids" loved every minute of it. The next day my brother wrote me an email that said, "It was a wonderful evening — the true meaning of Christmas." He's right.

72

Party Like It's 1970-Something

January 17, 2015

If you happened to be skulking about my neighbourhood at midnight a fortnight ago, peering into the brightly lit windows (and really, who among us hasn't?), you may have seen me splayed on the couch desperately trying to stay awake.

It was coming up on 1:00 a.m., which, these days, is a good two hours past my bedtime. I used to stay up for the news, but as my friend Wayne likes to say, what's the use of watching "moderately attractive people tell you what you already read on the Internet that day?" No, not me; most nights I'm tucked into bed at ten with a cup of Bénédictine-laced cocoa and a novel, typically held upside down.

But this night I was fighting narcolepsy, waiting for my daughter to arrive back from university for Christmas, or as we now like to call it, Vaguely Seasonal Festivities Which Cannot Be Named. We had divided duties — with my wife driving into Toronto to pick Ella up at Union Station and me sitting on the couch channel surfing. I think balance is what keeps a good marriage going.

This being Canada, the train was delayed — apparently someone forgot the engine — and the 11:00 p.m. arrival time had now stretched to midnight. With detraining and the trip home, I figured they'd be back at 1 a.m. at the earliest. I fought the inclination to change into my Spider Man pyjamas and fluffy slippers, a decision that turned out to be fortuitous. Around 1:30

a.m., I heard voices outside and wondered why my wife and daughter would decide to have a discussion on the front porch on a cold winter night.

Just then, the front door flew open and (I'm not kidding) a veritable throng of young people burst into the house. I thought it was a half-dozen of Ella's friends, but they just kept coming, and within minutes we had about thirty kids shaking off coats and boots, which is not that easy to do when you're carrying a two-four of Moosehead or a knapsack stuffed with clinking bottles, but they managed, the darlings.

My lovely daughter had neglected to inform me that all her friends had decided to greet her the moment she arrived — no matter what time that was.

I shook hands, was hugged, bear hugged, and kissed by her pals, both girls and boys, and within minutes had a beer pushed into my hand and was trading "first-term-away-from-home" stories. I think I even saw my daughter at one point, but I'm not sure. A tall girl with long brown hair — and that describes at least four or five people in the room — said "Hi, Pappy" and kissed my cheek. I chatted, drank several beers, and about 3:30 a.m. realized that the more than three decades that had elapsed since university had taken their toll and I needed desperately to pee, take an antacid, and go to bed. I think the party broke up about 4:00 a.m. (Actually, the next day this was confirmed for me by several neighbours who seemed to have noted the time precisely for some odd reason.) In the morning, I found a girl on the floor in Ella's room, a boy in the spare room, and four large young men fast asleep around our living room fireplace. They had covered themselves with any available pillow or throw blanket and I couldn't help but notice that one enterprising young man (and I wish I were making this up) had wrapped his shirtless body in what he thought was a blanket, but was actually a handmade Italian tablecloth my wife had picked up in Tuscany some years ago. There was no time for dry cleaning, so we used it on the dinner table that night regardless, though my daughter did note that "something smells a bit like Axe around here."

During her week off, between shopping, sushi lunches, and a half-dozen more parties, Ella did manage to find time to talk to me, on the last day before she left for Montreal. She was happy, healthy, and finding school "tough" but good. I told her I might visit her.

She said, "Call ahead. I don't want any surprises."

73

It's Been a Year: Food, Family, and Friends Have Wonderful Healing Powers

May 2015

It's been close to a year now and I haven't opened the bag.

My wife, who is good with these things, brought it out a couple of times and gently reminded me that I had to deal with it, to write the thank-you notes to people who made donations and dedicated masses.

I think I even brought the bag out to the cottage — not once, but twice — only to pack it back into the car after a week, unopened, unattended to.

It's just a plain, white plastic bag, but it's filled with the dozens and dozens of cards, letters, and notes that arrived in the days and weeks and months after my mom's death last year.

She died May 4, only a few days before Mother's Day, and this week marks a year since she passed.

As the day approached, my brothers and sisters and I sent tentative emails to each other. What should we do? Who knows really? Nothing seems quite right — not a party, certainly not a Mother's Day brunch, but then again, doing nothing doesn't seem right either.

Perhaps unimaginatively, we decided on the cemetery. We'd all meet there Monday on the anniversary of Mom's death and tend to the grave. I actually liked the idea. I don't go to the cemetery much, though I know some of my relatives do, especially my Aunt Louisa, who visits regularly. Personally, I don't much see the point, but I understand the urge. In fact, I did go, on my mother's birthday. It was a good thing to do, though I can't really explain why. It just felt right.

So, on Monday, we met at the graveside about noon. The day had begun warm and sunny, but now clouds were rolling in. It felt like rain. We hugged and then, with not much to say, we all got down to work, pulling weeds and clearing out some dead plants. My brothers brought soil and mulch, my sister Paula brought some pretty purple plants.

My sister Rosanne admitted the last few months had been hard — again — with the memories of my mom's last months flooding back to her. I said, for me, the summer had been the hardest, and with each month, I felt myself getting better. Not perfect, but better, and that was good enough.

Funny, how people process things. As the months went by, we made a point of calling and emailing more. Me and my brothers, Rob and Joe, started meeting for lunch. Nothing fancy, Portuguese or Vietnamese, just casual. We don't talk about Mom much and that's okay.

My sister Paula organized a cooking day in the winter, where we got together and made a regional specialty that my mother and her cousin Rosie were famous for — *olive ascolane*, or as we call them, stuffed olives. They originate in the town my mother's family is from — Ascoli Piceno, in Le Marche, Italy. They are a ridiculous thing to make, really. You have to hand peel olives and then carefully stuff the skin with a meat mixture, roll them in egg and flour and then egg and bread crumbs, and then fry them, and it takes three or four people virtually all day to make a batch. But we did it together and we talked for hours about Mom and cooking and our grand-parents and our childhoods and all the Christmases when we ate stuffed olives, savouring each one like a little gift.

People grieve differently, suffer in their own time, and heal in their own way. But doing it together can be helpful, and after the cemetery we went to Robert's for lunch. Our niece Alisa brought the new baby, named Grace, and we fussed over her. We ate cold cuts and fresh crusty bread and drank red wine and though we didn't talk about it much, it all reminded us of Mom and Dad and our dining room table, always filled with food and kids and laughter and love.

My sister said this winter we should get together and make lemon twists, my mom's favourite cookie. We hugged and said goodbye.

I went home and that afternoon, I pulled the bag out, sat in a chair, and carefully opened and reread every card, note, and letter.

It took me a year, but it was time.

74

Your Dad Does Not Want a New Necktie

June 20, 2015

It's not unlikely that at some point today, somewhere in this fair city, you will have a men's necktie in your hand.

If so, please put it down.

No matter how desperate you are, one day before Father's Day, to find a suitable gift, please do not purchase a tie.

Trust me as both a father of dubious parenting skills and a man who owns his fair share of neckties (and by "fair share" I mean enough ties to dress an infantry battalion and still have some left over for a couple of football teams): your father does NOT want a new tie.

He does not want a new tie because he still has not worn the one you bought him last year. It's funny how seldom an event arises that calls for orange-and-pink paisley neckwear. He also does not want one because he probably hates wearing a tie, and if by chance he's the rare guy who actually enjoys dressing up and donning a tie, he probably prefers picking them out himself, since the choice of tie is a highly personal and subjective matter. Like choosing a spouse, only much, much cheaper.

Your next idea might be to buy dad some tools. This is also a bad idea because I don't want tools and don't know how to use them. (That's for you, kids.) But even if your dad likes tools, it's highly unlikely he's been sitting around all year without a ratchet cleft (this could be a real tool, I have no idea) waiting for you to get him one on Father's Day. Let's face it, guys who actually know how to use tools buy their own. Nobody needs a half-dozen of the same Robertson screwdrivers, whatever that is exactly.

You could buy him some golf stuff, but if he's a pretty bad golfer — and really, is there any other kind? — your present is just a painful reminder of his last score.

No, I think it's time to reconsider Father's Day gifts. Here are some suggestions that will take you beyond the aftershave (also a bad idea) and necktie zone.

Take him out for dinner. The kind of dinner he likes. Don't fret if the place is called something like Charred Meat or Hoof and Snout. Just go and let him order the biggest slab of meat he wants.

Drop by some Sundays and watch sports on TV with him. Even if you pretty much hate sports on TV. Lots of dads like to "have the game on" all day Sunday, even if they are only half-watching it. You can sit around, drink a pop or a beer, and make offhand "sports comments" despite knowing almost nothing about sports. Try, "Do you believe how much they pay that bum?" or "They'll be golfing soon" (for hockey playoffs) or "They'll be playing hockey soon" (for golf — no, that one might not work). Anyway, you get the idea.

Stop in and do something you almost never did as a kid — like voluntarily cut the lawn, tidy up the garage, weed the garden, or clean the eaves. Do a job you know needs doing and that will give your dad a break.

Take him to the movies. If he's like a lot of dads, the last movie he saw in a theatre was *The Blue Max* or maybe *Bullitt*. Go to an action movie with him. The louder the better. Order popcorn. Guns, car chases, and empty calories. How do you beat that?

Stop in and ask for some advice. Even if you think you don't need it. (You probably do.) Good topics are work and jobs, buying a new car or house, and any aspect of raising kids. On the last one, he's likely to say: "I have no idea. Ask your mother." But your dad has a lot of experience — maybe even some wisdom — and he'll like that you asked.

Finally, there are two things you can give him that are free. Say "thanks," not for anything in particular, but for everything.

And tell him you love him. If that's a bit hard to get out, try adding "man" at the end as in, "I love you, man."

It seems to help.

75

Every Gardener Needs a Handy Wood Man

July 4, 2015

My wife and I have black thumbs. Not literally. Well, I hope not anyway. I try to wash regularly.

I mean, we're amazing with plants. And I use the word *amazing* as in the sentence, "Wow, it's amazing how fast that Easter lily died," or "I've never seen anyone manage to actually kill a cactus. They hardly even need soil or water. That's amazing."

And indeed it is. We're both excellent horticultural assassins. Plant killers. Anything green that comes into the house dies. It's so bad people won't visit on St. Patrick's Day.

Plants, flowers — hell, even those herbs you buy from the grocery store. They all mysteriously turn black immediately. This can cause some problems at the dinner table.

Guest: "Gee, what's this black stuff on the pizza?"

Me: "Oh, no worries. That used to be basil. Eat up."

With plants I think it's a case of extreme neglect coupled with hysterical diligence. This leads to neither of us watering our new plant for, say, a couple of months, until one of us looks at the now brown, crispy leaves of what used to be some kind of living vegetation and says, "Hey, I thought YOU were watering this."

Or both of us watering the plant daily, until one of us looks at the slimy, mossy mess in the pot and asks, "Can plants drown?"

The only exceptions are summer plants on the porch that nature seems to keep alive despite our actions, and in our backyard, where, ironically, everything is overgrown like crazy.

Recently, my brother-in-law came over because I told him our maple tree needed trimming. I'm okay with trimming a few words from a windy essay; trimming a tree is another matter. But Brent, sometimes known as "Woody" or "Wood Man," is an expert with a clipper, hedge trimmer, or chainsaw, if the situation demands it.

He walked down the driveway and looked at the overgrown mess of trees, shrubbery, and assorted vines, suckers, weeds, and other noxious plants that had virtually taken over our small yard and said, "You ever heard of pruning?"

"Yes, I have!" I said, brightening. "I'm not just pruning. I'm juicing. And I'm taking Metamucil. It all seems to help with, um, keeping everything 'moving.'"

"That's terrific," he said. "But I'm talking about pruning the garden, you know, actually trimming the shrubs and trees occasionally. Say, every ten years."

"I have no idea what you're talking about," I said. "I thought nature held itself in equilibrium."

At this point, my mind was racing back to grade eleven biology and the last science course I had taken in my life. "Yes! Homeostasis! That's it!" I took a moment to enjoy the fact that I had actually remembered something of value from high school. What would be next? Using the "cosine" in daily life?

At this point, I realized Woody was still staring at me.

"I figured if everything grew too much, I would just wait it out and a forest fire would clear the area."

"Great idea," he said. "In the meantime, we may have to intervene. I'll go get my saw, trimmer, and a ladder."

When he returned, he began hacking and sawing things out of the garden. Lots of things.

"These are suckers," he said, pulling out twenty-foot-high trees I didn't know were alive back in the cedars.

"You bet," I said, "Suckers for punishment from you."

Before long (and I'm not making this up), the yard was filled with piles of twigs, stumps, and branches of all kinds.

"I think you've got something growing on your Rose of Sharon," he said. This is one of the few plant names I recognize, so I went behind the shed to see what was there. I began pulling on a vine that had somehow wrapped itself around the poor bush. And pulling and pulling. "It's *The Day of the Triffids* back here! I need some help!"

We finally got the vine and all the rest of it out — two full loads to the dump — and the backyard looked amazing. (And not "amazing" in the dead way.)

Who says gardening is tough? All you need is a pair of clippers, a ladder, and a brother-in-law named Woody.

September Is the Real New Year

September 12, 2015

Some say April is the cruellest month, but I'll bet they never had to face September in Canada.

After the long, hot, hazy days of August, September slides in with a nice holiday weekend that stretches out the summer ever so slightly — and then sucker punches you back to reality.

Canadians are an industrious bunch (what other country would call a federal election in August?) but they do a pretty good job of kicking back in the summer. You can feel it once the weather gets really good — that collective sigh of relief from people who lived through eight straight months of wind, rain, and snow. But it really hits in the dog days of summer — mid-July and into August — when it seems like the whole country is on vacation. You get up early one morning and you notice something odd. The sound of car engines starting at the crack of dawn is missing. You walk outside and the street is bright and hot and utterly quiet. If you wander down to the closest main thoroughfare near your house, you see a street strangely devoid of cars. There are no traffic snarls. There isn't even traffic. It's like *28 Days Later* — without the zombies, unless you count teenagers forced to wake up early for their summer jobs.

Even the online world, which seems to never rest, takes a little break. You log on but the emails have slowed, perhaps a couple notes from friends, some spam, and not much, if anything, from work.

Where is everybody, you wonder? They're away — at cottages and camp-grounds, at provincial parks and waterparks, in trailers and tents, on beaches and boats — grabbing their piece of the summer that is always too short. And for a few fleeting weeks, if you're lucky, it's hot dogs and hamburgs, steaks on the grill, fresh corn on the cob and cold beer from the cooler, and warm nights on the dock or the deck, under a clear sky full of stars.

And then one evening in August, you can never quite remember precisely when, you start to feel it. The sunset comes a little faster and, when darkness falls, the night is still full of the buzzing hum of cicadas and crickets, but there's new hint of coolness in the air, perhaps a light wind cutting the humid stillness.

And then comes that nervousness echoing through time from a dozen or more years of Septembers, a dozen or more first days of school. It's hard to shake the feeling that September brings with it a kind of reckoning, and even decades after your final graduation — whenever that was — you can still sense it.

I always say that the real New Year isn't January 1, which never really kicks off anything new except for failed resolutions and the worst month of weather of the year, but rather September, when the summer ends and school starts and businesses everywhere click back into gear after the doldrums of July and August.

For me, it's the dreams that come at night and the anxious moments at dawn. You know the dream, the one where you didn't graduate from anything and you can't figure out why, or that you somehow missed the exam or, even worse, that you somehow, inexplicably missed a whole course and the final is today and you face the sickening realization that you don't know a bloody thing about the Renaissance or advanced algebra or the economy of Singapore and you are doomed to fail. Boy, that feeling will get you out of bed in the morning — you can't sleep anyway — and get you moving, making lists, checking your email, prepping for the inevitable return to school or work or both.

And so we stretch the days, savouring the long, lazy afternoons, pushing dinner later into the evening, eating outside by candlelight because the sun has suddenly dipped below the horizon, squeezing out every minute of the shorter days of the waning summer.

But try as we might to delay it, Labour Day comes and with it Tuesday morning, and we are back, one more glorious summer retreating quickly in time and memory behind us.

77

There's No Retirement in My Future

November 7, 2015

Recently, it has come to my attention that some of my friends are retiring.

I know this because they keep saying, "I'm retiring" over and over again and then laughing hysterically.

Though I am having difficulty lately multi-tasking — and by multi-tasking I mean breathing and then doing anything else at the same time — I did hear them.

Well, I sort of heard them. When we go out now, especially if it's a noisy restaurant, about half the evening is spent repeating ourselves. The conversation goes something like this:

Friend #1: "I'm retiring from work."

Friend #2: "You're rehiring what jerk?"

Me: "Don't rewire anything until you talk to my guy."

Friend #1: "No, no, I'm retiring. I'm done this year."

Friend #2: "Which ear? My right one's shot. I have a hearing aid, but I hate it.

Me: Ate what? We haven't even ordered yet.

Friend #1: Oh hell, never mind.

Me: You know, you should think about retiring. You're not getting any younger.

When they tell me that they're retiring, right from the bottom of my heart, I hate them. I'm kidding, of course. I don't hate them. It's really more of a deep, bitter jealousy.

I also can't really believe it. One minute we're sneaking two-dollar drafts at Paddy Greene's and the next thing you know people are talking about the end of their work life. Okay, so maybe a few decades have slipped by, but retirement? It seems insane.

Actually, according to my financial planner, who I see whenever I need to be plunged into a deep depression, the idea of retirement in my case is actually insane.

My problem, he pointed out, is "timing," explaining that "the 2008 financial crisis and the more recent market correction had a negative impact on your equity-heavy portfolio."

"What does that mean?" I said.

"It means that over the last fifteen years, your account has had a net growth of about $147. Minus my fees, of course." He estimated that, based on this growth pattern, I could probably retire "in 2057 or about thirteen years after your death — whichever comes first."

"Your other financial mistake," he continued, "was what we in the invest-ment game call 'ongoing negative income drains,' or 'children.'"

It turns out that, economically speaking, each child you have represents a lifetime expense of more than half a million dollars, give or take a couple of sets of braces and one or two fender benders.

"You," he said, "have three children or a net liability of $1.5 million. I, on other hand, have two beagles and a brand new Jaguar convertible. Also, here is a picture of my young and attractive wife. She used to be a lingerie model but had to give it up because she got too busty."

So, as I and my friends hurtle headfirst into our sixth decade, we find ourselves on the cusp between two amazing moments in life: impending retirement or the distinct possibility of a decade or more of being a Walmart greeter. Not that there's anything wrong with that — you get to meet a lot of nice people and the vest is pretty sharp. Me, I'm resigned to my fate. I was a late starter, spending several years after university trying to "find myself." My dad eventually succeeded in "finding me" — watching TV in the rec room — and told me to find a job. Being a good son, I snapped into action and only two or three years later, I did.

Anyway, all of that means that in practical terms, I'm probably a decade behind my pals who quickly embarked on successful business careers. The rest became teachers. Either way, they're both sitting on pensions that could choke a horse, though I'm not sure what the point of that would be.

Personally, I'd rather be part of the new movement that rejects the whole idea of "retirement" and would rather talk about moving to the next "phase" of my life.

Actually, I'd rather move on to a lawn chair with a good book.

Of course, I might have to do that in the outdoor furniture section of Walmart.

See you there.

78

If Pepperoni Is DEATH, I'll Take the Risk

December 5, 2015

Excuse me while I bite into this smoked meat sandwich. I'll be finished in a moment — perhaps in more ways than one.

Oddly, ever since the World Health Organization announced that salted, cured, and smoked meats were just slightly less dangerous than a plutonium hat, my wife has been feeding me a pretty much all-cold-cuts diet.

Yesterday, when she placed before me a plate full of sliced double-smoked kielbasa — for breakfast — even I began to get suspicious.

Of course, I'm kidding. My wife wouldn't even touch kielbasa, never mind slice it.

The point is the WHO made waves when they announced that red meat, and particularly processed meat, might be bad for you. Wow, shocker.

I mean, did anyone ever think that eating a five-inch-high pastrami sandwich was good for you? Let's face it, how could a "meat tower" with mustard on it be health food?

But let's look at reality. People all around the world eat smoked and cured meat. For the Italians, it's practically one of the four food groups — pasta, wine, salted pork, and cannoli.

Salted cured pork holds an esteemed position in Italy, just below the prime minister. If popularity ruled politics, a giant prosciutto would run the country. It is said, perhaps apocryphally, that the Inuit have one hundred names for snow, but it's true that Italians have at least as many for salted pork. Salami, prosciutto, cacciatore, salametti, pepperoni, pancetta, coppa, rotola, capicollo, bresaola, lardo, culatello, mortadella, salsiccia, soppressata, speck, sopressa, vitelline, and many others.

If people in Italy stopped eating cured meats, half their vocabulary would disappear!

One has to wonder how a whole country raised on *salumi*, or cured meats, even exists today. By the WHO's reckoning, pretty much everyone in Italy, except for the vegans there, should be dead by now. And even that one guy probably sneaks a slice of hot salami when no one's looking.

The WHO announced that salted and cured meats are a "level-one carcinogen," along with asbestos, smoking, and — I'm not making this up — plutonium. Personally, I can't remember the last time I had an asbestos sandwich, but I take their point. Or do I? The WHO's list of "Provable Carcinogens" includes (and again, I am not making this up): alcohol, salted fish, wood dust, being a chimney sweep, sunshine, house painting, air (well, okay, dirty air), working night shifts, eating fresh red meat, working at a steel foundry, birth control pills, and being a hairdresser.

If you add the list of "Probably Carcinogens" and then "Reasonably Anticipated to be Human Carcinogens" like "frying foods" and "mobile phone use," then pretty much everyone I know should be dead by now. After reading the list, I did think that I have been living a far more exciting and James Bond–like life than I realized. More than once I have drunk alcohol, stayed up late, breathed Hamilton air, and then fried bacon while answering my cellphone! I know, call me crazy, but hey, I like to live on the edge.

Then there's the reality that a lot of other stuff is probably carcinogenic: watching *Transformers* movies, hipster beards (come on, anything that ugly has to be dangerous), listening to Rush Limbaugh, that totally unidentifiable cream filling in Christmas chocolates, and headcheese. (Have you ever taken a good look at that stuff?)

Of course, once you get past the semi-hysterical headlines warning people that "Pepperoni is DEATH!," you get to the facts. Eating processed meats increases your relative risk of colon cancer by 18 percent. But the key fact to remember is that your absolute risk of getting colon cancer is already low — about 5 percent in your lifetime, so eating four slices of bacon or a hot dog a day raises that risk to — hold on to your BLT — 6 percent!

Me, I'm willing to risk the 1 percent increase so that I can have the occasional salami and prosciutto panino, a foot-long at The Arbor in Port Dover, a hot dog at a Tiger-Cats game, and a Schwartz's Deli Montreal smoked meat sandwich.

I might cut back on my chimney sweeping, though.

79

The Soundtrack of My Life

December 19, 2015

In 1974, when I was eighteen years old, Frank Sinatra came out of a short-lived retirement and embarked on a multi-city tour.

The closest concert was at Buffalo's Memorial Auditorium. I knew that this might be my last chance to see him.

While my friends were listening to Elton John and The Guess Who, I was playing albums like *Ring-a-Ding-Ding!* and *Only the Lonely*, over and over again. The music was what got me. It's not easy for a teenager to admit that he loves a singer who's older than his parents, but that was the case. So, on October 4, I scraped together all the money I had (plus some I borrowed from my mom) and quietly boarded a Greyhound bus bound for Buffalo. I had no ticket and no plan, except that I was determined to see Frank Sinatra sing. Live.

The concert was sold out. As evening approached, I hung around the Aud trying to cadge a ticket. The concert start drew near and I grew more and more nervous, worried that my journey had been for nothing.

As the smiling crowds gathered around the entrance, my hopes sank.

I was thinking about that October evening so many years ago because December 12 marked the one-hundredth birthday of Sinatra. December 12 is also the day I got married, and though I didn't plan that connection, it seems oddly fitting. Perhaps like a lot of people, I realized that in some ways, Sinatra's songs have always been a part of my life, the musical score behind the events and milestones that make a life.

At home, we were weaned on Sinatra. My mother knew the words to dozens of tunes made famous by him and she would sing them to us, especially at bedtime. Our lullabies were "In the Wee Small Hours of the Morning" or one of her favourites, "South of the Border."

Sinatra also got me out of some tight spots. When I was dating the woman who would become my wife, we came one evening to that conversation that inevitably arrives. You know, the "Where-is-this-relationship-going?" one. Caught off guard, I stammered, and then Frank saved me. I quietly started to half sing, "Let's take it nice and easy/ It's going to be so easy/ For us to fall in love/ Hey baby, what's your hurry?/ Relax and don't you worry/ We're gonna fall in love/ We're on the road to romance — that's safe to say/ But let's make all the stops along the way/ The problem now of course is/ To simply hold your horses/ To rush would be a crime/ 'Cause, nice and easy does it every time." Corny maybe, but it worked. Well, for a while, anyway.

Many years later, Sinatra would help mark another milestone, the retirement of my father-in-law. Pete loved Sinatra, particularly "My Way." So, to mark the evening, I retooled the lyrics of the song to recap his life — his business, his marriage, the early death of his wife, his struggles, and his happy second marriage. We called it "Pete's Way," and it was part of a slide show, and he loved it. Years later, when he lay in bed dying, surrounded by his children, we sang it to him one last time and, though he could not speak, the tears ran down his cheeks as we came to the final line, "You did it your way."

A few years later, when my mom died, we put together a slide show and her life flashed by us with Sinatra singing "Fly Me to the Moon."

That October evening long ago in Buffalo, I finally got in, paying one hundred dollars — a small fortune in 1974 — for a ticket a dozen rows from the front. It was an amazing night.

I would see Sinatra twice again, the last time in Hamilton in 1993 when he was in his seventies and I was married with two young children at home. Two years later, he would give his final performance, and the last song he would ever sing was "The Best Is Yet to Come."

In 1998, at the age of eighty-two, Frank Sinatra died. But his music lives on, his voice ringing through my home and those of countless others, his songs the soundtrack of our lives.

80

A Look Back at 2015, Benedetti Style

January 2, 2016

The end of the year and the dawning of a new one is a good time for sober reflection on the months that have passed.

Unfortunately, between Christmas celebrations, Boxing Day parties, and New Year's Eve bashes, sober anything, never mind reflection, is pretty hard to find.

Nonetheless, it's a good idea to take stock, as long as that stock is not Volkswagen shares.

This year saw its share of disruptions, scandals, blow-ups, payouts, pay-offs, takedowns, and crises — and that was just in Parliament. Across the country, it's been a mix of good and bad, and by bad we mean Drake's dancing in "Hotline Bling."

In politics, we saw the end of ten years of Conservative rule in Ottawa with the stunning election victory of the third-place Liberals. Experts attributed the turnaround to the fact that many Canadians, particularly young people, carefully considered the socio-political and economic issues and decided that Justin Trudeau's hair was "fabulous."

The Liberals were helped by a strong rumour that sometime during the campaign Stephen Harper had been replaced by a robot. This was bolstered by Conservative insiders who said they noticed the robot's hair "seemed more natural." The NDP made a crucial political mistake by forgetting the lessons of history — the first one being that no one with a beard has held public office in Canada since 1894. There was also the problem of Mulcair's seriousness. There were claims that someone actually saw him smile during the campaign, but later sources close to the leader confirmed it was "only gas."

After the landslide victory, the Liberals have enjoyed a brief "honeymoon" period, during which Trudeau's most substantial policy moves were:

1. appear in *Vogue*; and
2. wear brown shoes with a blue suit.

Canadians were thrilled with the idea of "sunny ways" — the phrase Trudeau used to describe the way forward for Canada. If the weather in December is any indication, he just may be on to something.

Political dust-ups included the Gas Plant Scandal, the Gas Bag Scandal (Mike Duffy), the Teacher Payoff, and the Hydro One Sale. All in all, it has been messier than a six-year-old's birthday party at Chuck E. Cheese — and almost as expensive.

In economic news, the Saudis turned the world economy upside down by offering oil for $2.95 a barrel, plus a free coupon to Arby's. The Canadian dollar dropped slightly, with experts saying the loonie is now on par with "those coins you get at arcades."

Cities, particularly Toronto, struggled with the arrival of Uber, the app-based driver service that is threatening to replace regulated taxi drivers. But no one is too worried because Nissan announced that robot cars will soon replace Uber drivers and Google announced that they would soon be replacing passengers with "things that upload to the cloud." Donald Trump then declared he would deport all immigrants from Uber or any other Muslim country, along with Mexicans, anyone who knows Hillary Clinton, and "people who smell funny." The news pushed Trump even further ahead in the polls, with Republicans declaring it's time for a president with "orange skin and a badger on his head."

In tech news, Apple released the Apple Watch, with some models priced at ten thousand dollars. The company did not release sales numbers, but one spokesperson said it was "more than six."

On the financial front, the stock market took a deep dive in August, wiping out most of the gains for 2015 and pushing my retirement date out to 2058. Analysts blamed China, and Donald Trump announced that he would deport "all Chinese people or anyone who even looks Chinese."

The year ended with: the Paris Climate Summit, with world leaders pledging to halt global warming or at least "think really hard about it;" U.S. President Barack Obama asking for gun control; and Pope Francis declaring unbridled capitalism the "dung of the devil." Donald Trump calls for all of them to be deported.

All in all, 2015 was quite a year and now that the New Year's cobwebs are clear, we should all look forward to 2016.

It's going to be warm — and it might even be sunny.

81

Grey Hair and Baggy Face?
How Did This Happen?

January 16, 2016

Excuse me while I take a moment to sit down. I'm feeling a bit faint.

It has dawned on me (once again, which is part of the charm of a progressively failing memory) that I am turning sixty. The precise date, if you must know, is today— sixty on January 16, 2016, a nice sequence of sixes which makes it easier to remember — even for me.

The central deep, philosophical question one asks oneself at this moment is: "Okay, how the hell did I get here?"

I mean, you know it's coming. You're not that dumb. At fifty, you realize that, with some luck, a decade will pass and you will still be standing, and you will become sixty. But in my perennially immature brain, the idea of being sixty is about as real as my chances of getting through any single night without peeing three times. In other words, zero.

I think of my grandfather — my mother's dad — in his sixties, a short, bald man wearing baggy pants and suspenders over his white sleeveless undershirt. In my mind, that's a man in his sixties — and I am not that man. At least, that's the inherent delusion of aging. The brain, sitting inside my skull and peering out through the eye holes is stuck somewhere between twenty-seven and forty-five, and always wondering, "Why do my friends look so old?" Of course, they're wondering the same thing about me.

When we all got together this Christmas at a local bar, as we do every year, I saw — in one brief moment — our table full of grey-haired guys dressed in sensible shirts as our twenty-something waitress saw us: a bunch of aging geezers out for an annual reunion of beer and nachos and bed by eleven. I had to laugh as I made my way — for the second time in an hour — to the bathroom to pee, the result of two drafts and a prostate the size of a potato. When did we become a troupe of old retirees and wannabe retirees in the local pub?

It's one thing to lie to yourself every morning as you gaze at your sagging and grizzled visage in the mirror, but it's another to ignore the photographic evidence of your decline. I had that breakthrough moment when we were at my nephew's recent wedding. There, they had a particularly new form of wedding sadism: the photo booth. In the strip of pictures spewed out by the infernal machine, my wife — a beautiful woman by any standard — looks great, blue eyes, chestnut hair, and red lips, smiling and youthful. It's the guy beside her that's a shock.

A grey-haired baggy-faced man who seems to be wearing a Groucho Marx nose-and-glasses set and oversized rubber Halloween ears.

And it's not just the visuals that confirm the march of time. I reluctantly admit the following realities of being sixty.

I now sleep with at least four pillows — two for my head, one under my sore right shoulder, and one between my legs. Rolling over requires two assistants and a fork lift.

I have to shave my ears.

I pee three times a night. Did I already mention that? I may have forgotten.

I forget things.

I'm tired at 10:00 p.m. and wide awake at four in the morning.

I can only hear half the words my daughter says.

My blood pressure is going up and my muscle mass is going down.

If I drink two martinis, my lips don't work.

But, the physical change (hell, let's call it what it is, the physical decline) is just the outward manifestation, the corporeal signpost of a much more important reality — the passage of time.

Being sixty is knowing, really knowing, there is now more behind you than in front, that the horizon of your life is, though distant, clearly in view.

That you have to be happy with, or at least resigned to, what you've done in life so far while being hopeful about what you still might do.

And mostly, I think, it's being happy that you're still here. Older, slower, perhaps a bit wiser.

But still here.

82

Zip Up. Pull Down Handle.

March 12, 2016

I'm not sure when young men stopped flushing their own pee.

But I know when I started noticing they had stopped. It was about a year ago now. I would walk into the washrooms at the university where I teach and see, as I stood peeing, that the urinals on either side of me were filled with various shades of urine.

Now you might say, "Well isn't that to be expected? What else would urinals be filled with?"

Yes, but normally people flush their urine away and what replaces it is clean, fresh water. Instead, I would find every urinal unflushed.

This would be the case whether I was in there in the morning, afternoon, or evening.

Often, when I was done, I would flush (naturally) and then walk along and flush all the other urinals.

Sometimes, a few students would walk in while I was doing this. They would stand and look at me, probably thinking to themselves, "I bet that guy has an arts degree" or "Man, I hope I don't have to tip this geezer."

But whatever they thought, what struck me was that they'd often, even after seeing that, pee and then walk away.

Without flushing.

I wondered about this for some time. I know what you're thinking: "Doesn't this guy have ANYTHING else to think about? Really?" But the issue seemed important. Men had been flushing urinals all around the world for more than a hundred years, and now, suddenly, they had stopped. Why?

I began to hypothesize. Maybe, warned over and over again about germs and hand-washing, guys had become "handle-phobic" and simply refused to touch anything in a public washroom. (Well, not anything, since they managed still, without assistance, to get their own, um, equipment out, and pee.)

But this idea seemed crazy. The answer to the germ problem is simple: 1. Pull down flush handle. 2. Wash hands thoroughly. I mean, you should be doing that anyway, right?

Maybe it's that they're all just, you know, "too busy" to flush. That they, in their digital, multitasking, hyper-connected lives, simply do not have time to flush. But that seemed too facile.

Young people have always been busy and stressed, but somehow we found the time to flush.

Perhaps, I thought, the almost endless accusations of "entitlement" were true. That these pampered, driven-to-everything, overprotected, and over-nurtured Millennials actually thought it was someone else's job to flush away their urine. "Hey, dude, I'm in a rush. Can you, like, get that?"

Or maybe they think "there's an app for that." Maybe they think their smartphone will flush the urinal.

Or perhaps it was just all my imagination.

But then about a month ago, I stood at the urinals and noted that someone had pasted small, neatly typed signs on each chrome handle. They read: "Please flush."

So, there it was. Evidence that what I had noticed was real! In a way, I couldn't believe it. I mean, you need a reminder to flush after you pee? What's next? Little signs saying: "Zip up your fly," "Wash your hands," and "Call your mother"?

I decided to investigate. I wanted to know if the staff who clean the washrooms across campus were responsible for these little "reminder" stickers. So, I walked over to the university services office and talked to the gentleman who oversees the maintenance crews. His name was Mark and he too had noticed the lack of flushing.

"It seems to come and go," he said. He was as puzzled as anyone as to why nobody seems to flush.

"It's not a lot of effort," he said. "I'm gonna guess it's laziness."

As for the little signs asking people to flush, he has no idea who put them there. "If you find out, let me know," he said, as I walked out.

I have not found out about the signs, but I have noticed that they aren't working. The urinals are still filled with pee. So, in the meantime, I just keep flushing them.

Hell, nobody else will.

83

Of Suits, Sadness, and Seasons

April 9, 2016

There was a time when if you walked into the newsroom wearing a suit and tie you didn't get very far before you heard: "Job interview or funeral?"

That was years ago and perhaps reporters are better dressed now than they used to be, but somehow I doubt it.

I was reminded of that this week when I went into the LCBO wearing a black suit and the cashier said, "You're all fancy today. Party?"

And I replied with a smile to take the edge off it. "No. Unfortunately, funeral."

I was on my way home after attending the funeral of my good friend Kevin's mother. It was, of course, sad, but as these things go, not that sad. His mom lived to ninety-three and had a full, rich life, emigrating from Ireland, marrying, and raising her two boys happily and well in Hamilton. I wondered to myself before the funeral whether she had outlived everyone, but dozens and dozens of old friends and neighbours came to pay their respects. There were tears and some laughs and hugs and it was nice. You know, as nice as these things can be.

I have found myself donning my black suit all too often of late. In the past few months, I've been to a handful of visitations and a few funerals. I used to laugh at my parents when they would say the only time they saw some friends was at weddings or funerals. Now I find myself, strangely, in the same shoes — literally a pair of conservative black toe caps I now keep polished in the closet for these occasions.

A few months ago, I was standing with my pal Cesare at the reception for his father, who died just after Christmas at the age of ninety-two. A good friend, he had helped me when my dad, and then my mom, died, and now I was returning the favour. Only a few months before that, we had stood together mourning the passing of his mother-in-law at the amazing age of ninety-seven. We agreed that we were lucky — blessed, really — to have our parents and our in-laws with us into our fifties and even sixties.

It's one thing to be grateful and another to be happy. I'd be lying if I said that this steady stream of funerals has not left me in some ways sadder than I used to be. No matter how long you have your parents, losing them is hard, and the hole they leave in your life, though expected and accepted, is large and their absence looms over you in ways that you didn't and couldn't expect.

And yet, as spring struggles to break through the stubborn remnants of winter, I look forward to donning a suit for different reasons. This spring there will be graduations from high school, college, and from university on all sides of the family. And on our fridge there are beautifully designed invitations for a wedding and a bridal shower, alongside tickets for the obligatory stag. And at Easter, we had my siblings together for a big dinner that almost didn't happen when my sister Paula suddenly took ill with the flu. My sister Rosanne stepped up on short notice and offered to host.

"We'll throw something together," she said. The something was a feast of spring lamb and a roast beef the size of a small car.

Of course, the absence of our mother and father was felt, but what filled the room that day were the kids, now all young adults, filling us in on their upcoming graduations and new jobs and exciting plans for the summer and beyond.

And the best news of all came near the end of the dinner when my sister was playing with the latest addition to the family, her granddaughter Grace, and called for the table to be quiet.

"What does Mommy have inside her?" she asked.

And Grace smiled across at her mother, Alisa, and said, "A baby."

There are tears and laughs and hugs. A new baby.

Outside, crocuses and tulips push up through the soil. It feels like spring.

84

These Beers Are a Little Too Crafty

May 7, 2016

Recently, I was having an end-of-term celebratory beer with my graduate students when I saw something unusual.

A student in the class, Sophie, was sitting in front of a bottle of beer with a very familiar label. I looked more closely and realized she was drinking Labatt 50.

I had not seen a bottle of Labatt 50, emblazoned with its classic green-and-red label, in years, and I think I hadn't seen anyone drinking it since my days at Paddy Greene's. And that, my friend, was a long, long time ago.

In fact, I thought "50" had disappeared, a casualty of changing tastes and changing times. Later, I asked Sophie, who is in her twenties, what she was doing drinking 50. She told me it was her grandfather's favourite beer, her dad's beer of choice, and now hers. "I've just kept the tradition going," she said.

I chided her about it being an "old guy" beer, and she said that's the going joke: "No one under fifty drinks 50!"

She laughed and told me that servers do a double-take when she orders a bottle, and many don't even know they carry it in their fridges, until she points it out to them.

It made me think back to the days when, like TV channels, there were about four beers in Canada. You know, Molson Canadian, Labatt Blue, Molson Golden, and Labatt 50. Sure, there were a couple of others, like Crystal or Old Vienna, Carling Black Label ("Hey Mabel, Black Label!")

and the beer every Italian grandfather drank, Molson Stock Ale. But mainly it was 50 or Blue and, in some bars, either one or the other, but not both.

I have to say, I kind of envied her conviction about brands. And I have to admit, I've jumped on the new micro-brewery-craft-beer bandwagon, but lately I'm wondering if it isn't all a bit too much. I mean, you ask the waitress, "What's on tap?" and seventeen minutes later she's still talking. Often, by the time she gets to the bottom of the list, I've forgotten what was at the top. Some of that is my memory, but some of it is the names they've come up with for these beers.

Is there really any good reason for calling a beer "State of Mind" or "Fracture" or "Smash Bomb Atomic IPA," or "A Miracle of Science" or (and I'm not making any of these up) "Saint of Circumstance"? I mean, it's not a bloody novel you're naming, it's just a beer. Besides, who the hell can remember all of that? The beauty of "Blue" or "50" or "Golden" was that, most of us, even after several pints, could still rally our brain cells to come up with one, single, word. Try pulling the name "Legendary Oddity" out of your skull after a few rounds or a hard day at the office. I can barely get the names of my three kids straight some days, and Mark or Matt or whatever his name is will attest to that. (Daddy's sorry.)

Besides, there's also the bar decorum issue, or what I like to call "Not sounding like a complete ass" when ordering a beer. Does anybody really say, "I'd love a cold 'Ransack the Universe,'" or even better, "May I have a bottle of 'Octopus Wants to Fight?'" Could anybody actually say that with a straight face?

Can you see a couple of firefighters coming in for a beer after shift and asking the waitress for a nice glass of "Bock Me Gently"?

On top of the names, there's also the small question of taste. Now, when I ask a server, "What's that beer like?" I get something like this: "It's very hoppy with hints of fresh grapefruit and orange peel and a touch of cloves." Okay, so is it an ale or a fruitcake? I'm confused.

Last week, I was at a local bar with some friends — all of whom were well over fifty — and the waitress walked us through the list of new craft beers and their names and their descriptions and finally one of the guys said, "Do you have anything that tastes, you know, like beer?"

Fifty, anyone?

85

Things My Father Told Me

June 18, 2016

Tomorrow is Father's Day and I'm sure my kids are busy right now completely forgetting that.

I don't blame them. My father used to say that all these days were invented by department stores to get people to go out and spend money on unwanted gifts for people they might not even like. National Boss's Day comes to mind.

My dad was particularly unimpressed by Father's Day, during which he would reluctantly accept our gifts with lines like, "If I wanted soap on a rope, I'd have bought soap on a rope" and other similar pleasantries. (Did anyone really want soap on a rope?)

Anyway, all of that got me thinking about my dad.

He died eight years ago this August, and for one reason or another, I think about him pretty much every day. I often recall the things he told us, at the dinner table or while we were out fishing together or just driving in the car. He wasn't big on fatherly advice in any kind of formal way, but a few things he said have stayed with me. Particularly, "If you don't stop horsing around in the back seat, I'm going to come back there and …"

Here are a few of my dad's words of wisdom.

1. "Get a government job. Nobody ever gets fired and the pension is great." I used to scoff at this as a young man, but there have been

many days when I wished I'd taken his advice. Two of my younger and smarter siblings did, and they'll soon be sipping mojitos on the beach while I'm looking at Freedom 95.

2. "You can only spend so much money on wine and women, but gambling is a bottomless pit." Odd advice from the man who taught us how to play poker, who bought the odd lottery ticket, and who enjoyed going to the casino now and again. But he was always careful, and when I read stories about people frittering away their life savings or embezzling funds from work to pour into slot machines, I remember his advice.

3. "Don't write on yourself. You'll get ink poisoning and die." This was always followed by, "I had a friend once who …" He would use this for all manner of calamity or dangerous activity. Growing up, we thought my dad had more dead friends than anyone on Earth. Then we realized that the friend — he usually called him "Pinko Pallino" — was the same guy who had, apparently, died a hundred different ways. Pinko had expired from ink poisoning, gone blind after staring at the sun, and, of course, drowned while swimming after eating. I have tried the same gambit with my kids around smoking, getting a tattoo, and driving a motorcycle — with mixed results. And I think they're on to Pinko Pallino.

4. "Never tell people what you make. Half will think you're bragging and the other half will think you're lying." To that I would add: and most people don't really care.

5. "Never book a one-week vacation. Always take two." With one week, he'd say, by the time you really relax, you have to start thinking about leaving.

6. "It's not what you make. It's what you spend." Everyone thinks a few thousand more will solve everything. It never does.

7. "Credit cards. If you don't have the money now, you won't have it in thirty days. Use them only in emergencies." Ah, if only I'd listened to that one.

8. "Everyone thinks their homemade wine is great. It's not."

9. "If you have something to do, do it today and get it off your mind." Words to live by.

10. "Bite off a little more than you can chew. And swallow hard." This is what he told me in 1989 when I went to him scared witless about buying our first house. He was right, of course. Although with interest rates running over 15 percent, I often needed a stiff drink to get it down.

To his list, I would add one more: "Listen to your old man."
I'm glad I did.

86

Convocation Miscalculation

July 2, 2016

If a person graduates from college and there's no one there to see it, did it really happen?

Better still, "Do you still have to pay?"

That's the existential question that we were faced with a few weeks ago. Well, the actual question we were faced with was, "How dumb can you get?"

Why?

Well, because somehow we missed my son Matthew's graduation. It's embarrassing to admit, but there it is.

I am a guy who routinely misses dentist appointments, drops meeting dates, and occasionally forgets to pick his kids up from school. (You haven't experienced real scorn until you've seen the face of your six-year-old who's been sitting in the hallway outside the principal's office for an hour and twenty minutes. Let me tell you, Dairy Queen stock went up that year.)

But this time, I can honestly say, it wasn't my fault. Well, not all my fault. We all knew that Matt was graduating on Tuesday, June 6. We were ready. We had even booked a nice restaurant in Kitchener to celebrate after the ceremony.

So, on Monday afternoon, we get a call from Matt's girlfriend, Laura, who seems to be having trouble talking. Finally, she says, "June 6 isn't Tuesday, it's Monday. It's today."

Unfortunately, we all figured this out right about the time the ceremony was actually starting. So, without the transporter from *Star Trek*, we were not going to be in Kitchener for any graduation any time soon. Matt and Laura came over and we all sat around the living room looking at each other. There wasn't really anyone to blame. We all had calendars, so exactly why no one figured out the date mix-up is beyond me. But we didn't. Our household does not function with the kind of precision normally associated with NASA. In fact, our house operates pretty much the way five-year-olds play soccer — we just run around in circles and hope something good happens.

Usually, that's fine, but this time even I was disappointed. My wife and I had really been looking forward to this graduation. Matt, our middle child, is a typical middle child — pleasant, well behaved, and a pleaser.

He said he liked school. Because he never complained, we didn't know things were bad. One morning, he pretended to have a stomach ache. My wife knew something was up, that school was causing him a lot of stress.

It took us a long time to figure out — in retrospect, much too long — that Matt had a "visual-cognitive decoding problem," which, in English, meant he didn't see letters and numbers like other people. And, of course, that made reading and writing and arithmetic very, very hard. We got him tested and found out what we already knew — he was a smart, talented, nice kid who needed some help. He went through middle school in a separate class with a small number of students and a great teacher named Mrs. Toth.

In high school, he had an independent education plan and some outside tutoring. Even with that, it wasn't easy, and honestly, we only later realized that we didn't know the half of it. Matt kept most of that to himself.

But he graduated and, after travelling and working in Europe for two years, he came home to go to school. He had decided on woodworking technology and we were thrilled.

And so we come to June 6. We knew how hard he had worked to succeed in college and we really wanted to celebrate that. We had looked forward to the whole gown-and-cap ceremony.

"It's not that big a deal," he said. "I really don't care that much about the ceremony, to be honest," he said. "I think it means more to you than to me."

And I realized he was right. It was his graduation, his milestone, not ours, and it was his to celebrate any way that he wanted.

Our kids' accomplishments — and their missteps — are their own. Taking too much credit — or blame — is perhaps not such a good idea.

So, we all went out for tacos and beer. Because that's what Matt wanted. And it was nice.

87

Whatever Boat You Float, Fishing Is Fun

July 16, 2016

It is mid-July and Canadians everywhere are engaging in one of the great traditional summer activities that has been practised for centuries and that defines us as a nation — beer drinking.

Sorry, I meant to type "fishing." I was just thinking of beer drinking because it's the summer and I'm Canadian.

Nonetheless, the correct answer is fishing.

Now, when you think of fishing you may imagine a man smoothly paddling across a glassy lake, his vest festooned with hand-tied flies, gently arcing his line to a beckoning trout. Later, you might wonder what "festooned" means, but that will pass. Or you may see a guy standing on a sleek bass boat, a huge black Merc on the back, a tiny trolling motor on the front, expertly casting into the reeds in search of bass.

If you are seeing those scenes, what I can assure you is that you are not seeing me.

I am up at the Thousand Islands on the beautiful and majestic St. Lawrence River standing on the *Wet Wiener*. The *Wet Wiener* is a boat my brother-in-law John generously lets me use to go out fishing in the mornings. It is a curious cross between a metal pontoon boat and a small garbage scow. To complete the look, it has a steel half roof under which sit several white plastic deck chairs. John drove it up from his home in Florida to help shuttle people and supplies back and forth to his island cottage.

By now, you are probably asking yourself, "What kind of nut takes a metal pontoon platform boat out fishing?"

We'll get to that, but you are even more likely asking why is this boat called the *Wet Wiener*? And do I really want to know?

The boat was originally the brainchild of John's two boys, who envisioned the greatest summer job of all time and, perhaps, the seeds of a worldwide franchise. They cleverly thought that if they put a barbecue on the deck of this pontoon boat, they could travel up and down the beaches and canals of Florida, selling boaters and tourists freshly grilled hot dogs and cold beer. Hence the name, the *Wet Wiener*. Unfortunately, short-sighted regulators decided that having a flaming barbecue fuelled by several propane tanks on a moving vessel amid swimming tourists was perhaps not the safest idea in the world. Nonsense, I say. Without this kind of American ingenuity, we would never have had high-risk breakthroughs like the space program or jalapeno-flavoured nachos.

In any case, Florida's loss was my gain. Not only can I take the boat out, but the *Wiener* is perfectly designed for my particular set of boating skills. And by "particular," I mean "really bad." After watching me try to dock a boat, no sane person would lend me their fibreglass motorboat unless what they wanted to come back was something that could later be used as a large, leaky planter. But John is okay with letting me "skipper the *Wiener*" or "take out the Hot Dog" or any number of expressions my wife hates, because not only is it made out of metal, but it has a thick rubber lip that goes around the whole boat, pretty much making it a floating carnival bumper car. This means that when I expertly guide the *Wiener* straight into wooden docks or the occasional rocky ledge, I can return it pretending nothing happened and it's none the worse for wear.

That's why most mornings I get up early and head out onto the glassy river to try and catch some bass. I admit that I am not the most skilled fisherman, nor do I look the part.

So, if you are out early on the river, what you might see is a man dressed in pyjama bottoms (weather depending), a ratty golf shirt, and a baseball cap on backwards, balancing himself on a bobbing pontoon raft, trying to get a worm on his line without impaling himself with a hook and ending up in the ER.

You will also see a guy having a ton of fun.

And, sometimes, I even catch a bass.

88

Do I Need to Get a Man Bag?

July 30, 2016

Last week I received an odd email from a colleague in London. This was the subject line: YOUR PHONE IS AT FORTINOS.

This seemed strange because I knew I had my phone right in my ... oh, wait, no, well, I had it here a minute ago ...

She informed me that she had tried to call me, only to have my phone answered by a young woman saying I wasn't there but had left my phone with her.

At that point, I felt lucky my wife had not called me. You can see, I'm sure, how this kind of thing could get a guy into trouble.

The young woman was, of course, the checkout person I had been chatting with while busily bagging my groceries and leaving my personal items behind.

I wish I could say that this was the first time this has happened, but that would cause employees at Fortinos to blow their morning coffee out their noses. I've been to the Customer Service counter so much they greet me with, "What is it this time?" I've left behind my glasses, my wallet, my phone, and occasionally even some of my groceries. I've left stuff in my cart, forgot stuff at checkout, and dropped stuff in the parking lot.

I now view virtually every outing as an opportunity to either: lose something; forget something; or buy the wrong something. If only one of these happens, I see the trip as a success, as long as I drive the right car home.

My friends have a complex psychological theory for why this happens to me. "You're an idiot," they say. Naturally, I prefer my theory: that people (okay, older people) are carrying too many things around. Right now, I cannot leave the house without a wallet, keys, a cellphone, sunglasses, and case, some loose change for parking meters, and a bottle of eyeglass cleaner. The eyeglass cleaner is so that I can clearly see what I've lost during the outing.

Carrying this much stuff around is a challenge. If you put it in your pockets, you look like either you've put on ten pounds or you're a very bad shoplifter. If you keep it in your hands, you can't really do any shopping without putting something down. Once you do that, there's an even chance you'll arrive home with a new pair of underwear but no phone — or vice versa.

What's the solution? I've noticed a couple of my pals seemed to have figured it out. Recently, we met a friend and his wife for breakfast and I saw that he had a small, black leather thing that looked suspiciously like a purse.

"It's not a purse," he said. "It's a shoulder bag."

"Then how come it's not on your shoulder?" I said, unhelpfully. "It's on the table, so maybe it's a table bag?"

We haven't been invited back out for breakfast.

The issue for guys, it seems, is not the bag per se, but rather what exactly to call it.

Some men prefer "messenger bag," except they are not messengers. You could call it a "rucksack." You could if you were a character in a Thomas Hardy novel. You might use the new term "café bag," but only if you think it's a good idea to be thought of as a total urban poseur. And you could, unwisely, call it a "murse," but be prepared to be "mursilessly" mocked.

My friend Dave brought his "man bag" on a recent cottage weekend. It was small and black with little handles.

"It's a tote bag," he said.

"It looks like a purse made out of an old scuba suit," I replied.

"It's neoprene," said Dave. "I keep all my stuff in it."

"Cute," I said.

Of course, I mislaid my phone for several hours, worried about my keys, and lost my glasses twice, while Dave had all of his stuff at the ready all weekend.

Cute indeed.

So, I'm considering a bag. Maybe it's time to give in and stop shlepping all my stuff around everywhere I go. Maybe I'll get a murse.

My only question is: do I have to buy matching shoes?

89

School Daze

August 27, 2016

Every year about this time thousands of young people prepare to head off for the greatest adventure of their lives.

A ride on the giant roller coaster at Canada's Wonderland while high on medical marijuana.

Just kidding.

They're actually preparing to go away for their first year of university.

Which, when you come to think about it, is not all that different from the Canada's Wonderland thing.

But in any case, many of these exuberant teenagers are seeking advice about their foray into undergraduate university studies. And by many, I mean "none" since every teenager I have ever met already knows everything and wouldn't listen to a parent or any other old geezer even if the rear of their jeans was in flames and you were standing there holding a fire extinguisher.

You: "Care for a spray?"

Them (feigning boredom while smoke billows around them): "Whatever."

I know this from personal experience because I tried it with my daughter a few years ago when she was heading off to Montreal for school.

"You know, honey," I said gently. "I actually went to university and might have a few tips for you."

"Oh god, Dad, that was like a million years ago. You didn't even have computers, right?"

"Well, yes that is right, but …"

"Ha, ha, ha…. You kill me. What, did you write on clay tablets? Did everyone carry around papyrus rolls and wear togas? Ha, ha, ha …" (Leaves room wiping away tears.)

I would have admitted that the toga part was at least kind of accurate, since the mid-seventies was the apex of toga party madness, but those stories were better left untold, now that I think about it.

So since none of the young people in my extended family will listen to me, I've decided to do what all parents my age do, just walk around the house talking to myself.

> Dear First-Year Student:
> You are on the cusp of one of the most amazing experiences of your life.
>
> Frosh Week.
>
> Just kidding, although that can be quite something — a bit like marine boot camp crossed with Mardi Gras, but with more throwing up.
>
> No, you have been given the wonderful opportunity of spending your parents' hard-earned money, sorry, I mean spending the next four years learning about culture, art, science, history, and politics. Some of that may even happen at school.
>
> To make the most of it and to prevent your parents from becoming eternally bitter about the vacations they missed and the lousy old cars they had to drive to save for your education (Not me, of course, I really enjoy driving a dented 2009 Impala that makes me look like an under-cover police officer. I do.), please do the following:
>
> 1. Go to class. That's right. Actually go to your lectures. If your parents wanted you to sit around playing video games and eating Doritos, they would have left you in your room.
> 2. Go to class. Yes, I'm saying it again. Woody Allen once said that "80 percent of success is showing up." He was

right. The online video, the class slides, your friend's notes, are no substitute for actually listening to a living, smart person, even if they are wearing a really bad sports jacket.

3. Be there. If you are in the lecture, then BE in the lecture. Don't be on your cellphone texting your pal about last night's bong party. Forget Facebook, Snapchat, and Instagram for forty-five minutes. They'll be there when you get out of class. Trust me. And forget tweeting funny comments about the prof on Twitter. No one is reading your feed anyway.

4. Try actually READING the readings. I know, it's "totally pages and pages of, like, words," with no video clips or music or anything. Dude, it's so, like, boring. I know, but if you actually take some time and read the stuff, you might discover that it's full of "ideas" and that can be a thrill. Not like shotgunning a tallboy of Molson Ice, but a thrill nonetheless. And, usually, you don't barf later.

5. Have fun. Of course, have fun. But if fun is all you want, the trip to Wonderland is a lot cheaper. And you'll probably barf anyway.

90

Reflections on the Long Road of Parenting

August 13, 2016

It's nice to be able to say at sixty that I experienced a new "first."

Last week, I went to my first bar mitzvah. Our very good friends, Wade and Aviva, invited us to the celebration of their eldest son, Ben's, transition into manhood. We were honoured to be there.

It was wonderfully different and, at the same time, comfortably familiar. As a boy of thirteen, I went through what Catholics call Confirmation, and much later we guided our three somewhat reluctant children through the same ceremony, so I was well acquainted with the general idea. Every culture and religion seems to have such a ceremony, a rite of passage captured in ritual and celebration that marks the step from childhood to adulthood for boys and girls. It is the moment when you leave behind childish things and assume responsibility for yourself and your actions.

For us, the bar mitzvah was a wonder. A swirl of colourful shawls, the tefillin and yarmulkes worn by the men, the stunningly ornate Torah and the dizzying recitation of Hebrew prayers mixed with the beautiful, often haunting singing of the cantor.

It was a friendly, warm, and busy affair, filled with serious ceremony, a touch of humour, and even candy throwing. There's something you don't see at a Confirmation.

But what struck us most were the speeches, first young Ben, who thanked his parents and family and who promised to work hard and be honest and true. And then by his father, Wade, who spoke to his son about the future. He told him that his young life was like a river, not unlike the one upon which their family spent summers up north, a winding and variable thing, marked by both calm pools and rushing rapids, by eddies and currents and even waterfalls, by places demanding courage and skilful paddling and others that called for caution and, perhaps, a portage. And he told his son that the banks of the river, watching and guiding him, were his parents and siblings and grandparents and his family and friends, all there for him along the ceaseless flow of his life.

After the party, I thought about Wade's beautiful words as we walked the few blocks home in the afternoon sunshine. I was elated by the ceremony and then sad, suddenly and unexpectedly aware of how much of the river of our children's lives had passed us now and how much of my own life had been lived, lived well and richly for sure, but gone, receding into the past.

When we got to the house, our two sons were there loading up the car. On this very same day, our eldest, James, was moving out, a decision he had announced to us some weeks earlier. We were pleased of course and, to be honest, also relieved. No more reprimands about messy rooms, no more arguments about noise or cigarette butts or dirty dishes. No more. Now, he would live life his own way and learn as he went along. But as they packed the last load and we stood awkwardly in the driveway, I was anything but happy. My wife hugged our son, who though only moving a few blocks away to join his younger brother in a house they were renting, was nevertheless "leaving," and we both felt it.

I did what most dads do — asked him if he needed anything, loaned him a few twenties to "tide him over" until his paycheque came in, and stood there like a fool. Then James said, "Thanks for letting me live with you for twenty-seven years," and leaned in to give me a hug.

We watched them drive away, left there standing on the sidewalk as a huge part of our life came to a small, quiet end on a sun-filled, summer afternoon.

Later, I realized that my sadness was tinged with something else. It was envy. I envied Wade and Aviva, envied them the coming years, the laughs and tears and successes and challenges they would have raising their kids. And I mourned the passing of it for me. That night, late, I texted my son a note: "Congrats on your move. Happy for you. Gonna miss you."

And he wrote back, "Gonna miss you, too, Dad. Thank you."

Acknowledgements

No project, least of all a book, comes together without the help of a lot of people.

The essays in this book were written over several years and many people helped inspire, encourage, and contribute to their creation. If I miss anyone in this list, I apologize in advance.

I'd like to thank my good friend Dave Estok, who, in his role as editor-in-chief of *The Hamilton Spectator*, asked me to start writing for the paper again and offered me a regular column.

That offer might not have come if the *Spectator*'s editorial page editor, Howard Elliott, had not approached me some years earlier to write a monthly essay for a magazine the paper was launching called *Ruby*. Those essays were in many ways the model for the columns I would write for the paper.

Every writer needs a good editor or, in my case, a whole team of good editors. I'd like to thank Rob Howard, who edited the column for many years, caught my dumb mistakes, and provided a slew of very funny head-lines. Many other editors have cleaned up my errors over the years, including Mike Bennett, Aviva Boxer, Lee Prokaska Curtis, Tawny Sinasac, Cheryl Stepan, and, overseeing the team, Howard Elliott. Thanks to all the readers of the column in the *Spectator* and especially to those who have written me personal emails and letters. I appreciate each and every message sent.

Of course, there would not be a book at all without the amazing people at Dundurn Press. First, thanks to Kirk Howard for okaying the project and supporting it through some rough patches, to Carrie Gleason, Margaret Bryant, Michelle Melski, Kathryn Lane, my editor Allison Hirst for her hard work in selecting the essays and giving them a shape, and to Courtney Horner and the design team for the wonderful book cover.

Writing is, by definition, a solitary pursuit, unless you have friends like Kevin von Appen and Wayne MacPhail, with whom I have written for many years on many projects. Their guidance and advice has been invaluable as has been the support of their wives, Diana von Appen and Barb Ledger. I'd like to especially thank Wayne, who helped me put together the proposal for the book and gave me the gift of a very funny title for it.

In the same vein, I'd like to thank my friend Wade Hemsworth for his ongoing support, his regular, lovely notes about the essays, and his sage advice on writing — and on life.

The essays in this book are the product of my interaction with my friends, many of whom appear in the work. These columns would not exist without their antics and their support, so thanks to Ron and Heather Gelens, Kevin and Susan Grantham, Steve and Lori Higgins, Paul and Vic Higgins, Adriaan and Nancy Korstanje, Scott and Juliette Lamb, John and Liane Ormond, Mike and Karen Simpson, Jean Mullens and Andy Coburn, Allan Meyer and Kelly Watt, and Dan Klick.

A special thank you to my pal Cesare DiDonato and his wife, Vicki, for their long, ongoing friendship and constant stream of supportive emails and comments about my work. And to our lovely friends Doug Brady and Carol Shea, with whom we have shared our lives for decades.

My colleagues at work — James Compton, Wendie Crouch, Mary Doyle, Mark Kearney, Meredith Levine, Cliff Lonsdale, Cindy Morrison, and Ella Young — who have read many of these pieces and offered support and encouragement.

My friends and neighbours have also played a part in all of this, so thanks to all the good people on Flatt Avenue, Gord and Anne Howarth, Phil and Marnie Denton, and Paul and Maria Doesburg, for their supportive emails, as well as the members of my all-guy book club — John Dean, Bruce

Goodbrand, Gord Howarth, Neil Jones, Graeme Luke, Keith Mann, and Bob Savage — who also live in the hood.

A special thank you to my friend and long-suffering neighbour two doors down, Dave Malcolm, who is not only the inspiration for some pieces, but always greets the writing with grace and good humour. Thanks, too, to his wife, my friend Annette Aquin, who allows us to sit in the yard and drink gin instead of doing lawn work.

Thanks go out to my wife's large family, which has become like my own family — her father, Pete Flaherty, now gone, but such a big support always, his wife, Fran, and her children, and my wife's brother and sisters and their spouses and their children: John and Penny Flaherty, Shelagh Flaherty and Tony Gismondi, Sandy Flaherty, Barbara Flaherty and Tyson Haedrich, and Patti Flaherty and Roger Lake, who have generously allowed me into their homes and cottages and into their lives. A special thank you to Brenda Flaherty and Brent "Woody" Wood, with whom we share a cottage and much else and who have put up with me at close range for a long, long time.

All of this would be a lot harder without the support of my own wonderful family — my mom, Mary, and dad, Ugo, who are gone now, but remembered every single day, and my brothers and sisters, Rosanne and her husband Joe Cascella, Paula and Derrick Luck, Joe and Gabriella Benedetti, Robert and Anne Benedetti, and all their kids, who have shared their lives with me and who have generously allowed me to write about them.

This book would not even remotely exist without my three children — James, Matthew, and Ella — who have inspired me every day and inspired much of the work in this book and have taken it all in good humour and with unstinting support. I love them more than I can ever say.

Finally, there would be none of this without my wife, Marni, whose love and unwavering support has made everything possible. She has been my first reader, my guide, my better judgement, and my friend. This book is for her.

(But I'm still not wavering on the dog thing.)

Paul Benedetti
2016

Of Related Interest

Cottage Daze
James Ross

Cottage Daze celebrates life at the cottage where the cottage is the main character, and family, friends, pets, and fellow cottagers are the supporting cast. Whether writing about cottage routine ("First Ski," "Of Mice and Men," "Cottage Guests"), cottage tasks ("Splitting Wood," "Boat Launch"), nature ("A Gathering of Loons," "The Sting," "Autumn Spell"), cottage fun ("The Cottage Duel"), or cottage touchstones ("Start the Day," "Bonfire," "The Perfect Storm"), the stories are told with humour, compassion, insight, and nostalgia.

Who doesn't remember sitting in a frigid lake, trying to help a youngster get up on water skis for the first time, launching a boat while the whole world seems to be watching, or getting caught up in a nest of wasps? This collection of stories, elegantly organized into four seasons (spring, summer, autumn, and winter), will make readers laugh, cry, and long to be at the cottage a "must have" for every cottage bookshelf.

The Sound of One Team Sucking
Christopher Gudgeon
With Tavish Gudgeon, Joey Mauro, and Yusuf Saadi

We've all heard it. The sound of one team sucking. Our team. The Leafs. It starts as an almost imperceptible hum, a month or so after the home opener, once the shine of the new season wears off, building in intensity with each defeat until the sound explodes like the noise a star might make if you ripped its heart out. Fact is, being a Maple Leafs fan is a kind of addiction: irrational, compulsive, dependent. You can't just quit cold turkey. You need help …

And that's where *The Sound of One Team Sucking* comes in. Think of it as your own portable support group, designed to accompany you through another disappointing season (plus draft day!), and guide your recovery as you strive to live a more emotionally and spiritually balanced life. Written by Leafs addicts, *The Sound of One Team Sucking* is a hilarious meditation on the futility of Leafs fandom.

🌐 dundurn.com   📷 dundurnpress
𝕏 @dundurnpress   📌 dundurnpress
📘 dundurnpress   ✉ info@dundurn.com

FIND US ON NetGalley & Goodreads TOO!

🏛DUNDURN